Richard Osborne
FREUD FOR BEGINNERS

PUBLISHED BY

Zidane Press.
9, Tremlett Grove,
London, N19 5LA.

DISTRIBUTED BY

Turnaround Publisher Services Ltd.
Unit3, Olympia Trading Estate Coburg Road, Wood Green
London N22 6TZ
Phone : +44(0) 20 8829 3019

Richard Osborne

Sigmund Freud is one of the most famous Doctors of all time, not always for the right reasons however.

Many people have heard of Freud but often they do not know his work. We are going to look at his work and at why he is famous. Like Freud we will start with the ordinary and obvious and work our way into the more difficult and murkier bits.

First of all Freud, like most people, had parents. In the long run this was to prove very significant in the intellectual revolution that Freud brought about. He basically changed for ever the way we think about human relationships. This is a fairly major thing to have done, modern man and woman would not be the same without it.

Freud was born in 1856 to Jakob and Amelia Freud, an older father and a younger mother. He was Amelia's number one son and firm favourite. His father was a not very successful wool merchant but he lived to a ripe old age, and had three marriages and plenty of children. This produced some complications for the young Sigmund. This is also where the famous aphorism that the child is father to the man (let alone the woman) comes in. Choosing your parents is an important business!

There were four complicated and significant things about Sigmund's childhood.

1) His mother adored him and always knew he would be great.
2) His father was not a success, producing hardship and trauma.
3) His family was Jewish, in an anti-semitic culture.
4) All his extended family wanted him to do well, encouraging him to be ambitious.

These factors were to shape Freud's outlook in significant ways, indeed many people argue that Freud's work and his own psychological make-up are inseparable.

Scenes from an infant life

When Freud was born his father already had two grown up sons, one of them, Emmanuel, was married with children. Freud was born an Uncle and his first playmate John, who was a year older than him, was his nephew. His mother was more or less the same age as his brothers. These childhood conundrums certainly gave an impetus to Freud's later interest in the enigmas of human emotions.

Freud was always proud of his Jewishness, despite the fact that neither he nor his family were religious in the practising sense. His nursemaid was a devout Roman Catholic which helped as well. Later Freud maintained a deep interest in biblical history and religion, again quite possibly motivated by these childhood experiences.

In 1860 the family moved to Vienna, mainly for financial reasons. Freud was to live there for the next 78 years, so Vienna can be called his home town. Freud worked incredibly hard at school in Vienna, often coming top of the class. He read all the time, learnt languages and got his own room in the crowded family flat. The girls shared.

Did Vienna influence Freud? Was he a product of bourgeois Vienna and its general culture? Well of course he was, but he was much more than that. He was a 19th Century white middle-class male but he was also a radical thinker who upset a lot more than the apple-cart. Freud saw himself as an outsider in Viennese culture in any case, as a Jew in an anti-semitic culture.

The four main phases of Freud's work

Studies in hysteria from private practice (1886) until the break with Breuer (1895)

Self-analysis and formulation of major principles (1895-1899)

Id psychology, first system of psychoanalytic psychology (1900-1914)

Ego psychology, extension and reworking of earlier ideas, 1914-1939

AS A PHILOSOPHER, I'D LIKE TO ASK ABOUT THE SORT OF INTELLECTUAL BACKGROUND THAT GAVE RISE TO PSYCHO-ANALYSIS. FOR EXAMPLE, SOCRATES SAID "KNOW THYSELF" — IS THAT WHERE IT COMES FROM?

AN ARCHAEOLOGIST?

NOT EXACTLY. ALTHOUGH I WAS MUCH INFLUENCED BY THE GREEKS AND BY BIBLICAL HISTORY, I SOMETIMES FELT LIKE AN ARCHAEOLOGIST...

WELL, A KIND OF DIGGING AROUND IN THE HUMAN PSYCHE FOR IMAGES AND CLUES THAT WILL ALLOW ME TO UNRAVEL THE MYTHS AND MYSTERIES OF HUMAN CULTURE, MUCH OF IT HIDDEN BELOW THE SURFACE.

IS IT NOT PECULIAR THAT YOU STARTED WITH PHYSIOLOGICAL EXPLANATIONS OF MENTAL DISEASES AND ENDED UP WITH A "TALKING CURE" THAT IS CONCERNED ONLY WITH MENTAL PHENOMENA?

SO WHY DO YOU HAVE THIS TERRIBLE REPUTATION?

I WENT WHERE SCIENCE LED ME, TO DISCOVER THE UNCONSCIOUS AND THE COMPLEX WAY IN WHICH THE HUMAN PSYCHE OPERATES, I WAS AN EXPLORER OF THE MIND AND OF THE ILLNESSES THAT AFFLICT HUMAN BEHAVIOUR, NOTHING MORE, NOTHING LESS...

WHAT I DISCOVERED WAS IN ONE SENSE SCANDALOUS AND I SUFFERED FOR MY DARING ... HAD I BEEN AROUND EARLIER THEY MIGHT HAVE BURNT ME AT THE STAKE, AT LEAST THE NAZIS JUST BURNT MY BOOKS ...

So how did Freud get from hard-working school-boy to the Unraveller of dreams and the founder of Psycho-analysis?

He decided to become a Doctor, then a researcher.

He went to the University of Vienna medical school in 1873 then into the research laboratory, where he searched for the gonads of eels because everybody thought they didn't have any.

He cut up hundreds of them in a thorough and methodical manner that was to characterise all his later work. He was already a proper scientist, by which we mean he collected evidence and attempted to explain the facts in a manner that was rigorous and methodical.

Freud studied under Ernst Brücke who, like most other people at the time, was heavily influenced by determinism. Freud probably switched from research to private practice because he wanted to make money and marry his girlfriend Marthe Bernays.

PS He found the gonads.

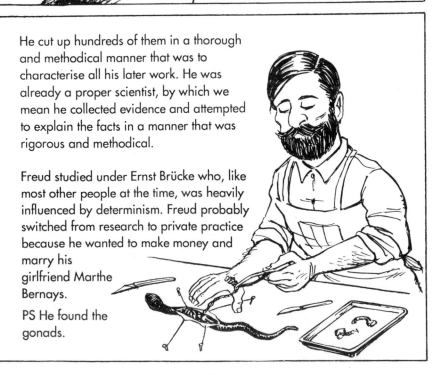

Freud and psychoanalysis are inseparable. All forms of pyschoanalytic thought go back to Freud, whether through agreement or disagreement. In some ways his original thought has been altered, superseded, developed and distorted out of all recognition, but his work is still the foundation on which everything rests.

Freud coined the term psychoanalysis in 1896 after a long struggle to work out his ideas on the causes of neurosis and other mental disorders. As we approach the first hundred years of psychoanalysis the question will be just how successful has it been as a therapy and as a theory of the human mind?

We can say that psychoanalysis roughly consists of three areas:

1) A mode of therapy aimed at relieving distress and based on theories of the unconscious and its interpretation.

2) An overall theory of how the human personality develops and functions.

3) A set of theories about how man and society function, based on the importance of the first 2 for understanding civilization.

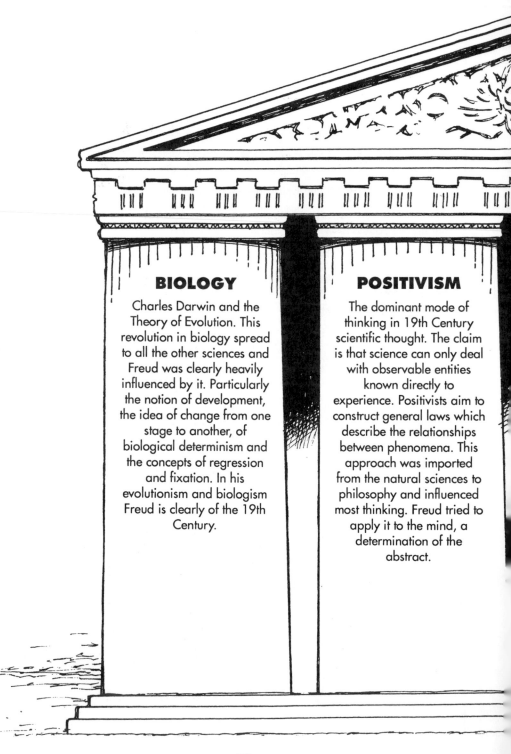

BIOLOGY

Charles Darwin and the Theory of Evolution. This revolution in biology spread to all the other sciences and Freud was clearly heavily influenced by it. Particularly the notion of development, the idea of change from one stage to another, of biological determinism and the concepts of regression and fixation. In his evolutionism and biologism Freud is clearly of the 19th Century.

POSITIVISM

The dominant mode of thinking in 19th Century scientific thought. The claim is that science can only deal with observable entities known directly to experience. Positivists aim to construct general laws which describe the relationships between phenomena. This approach was imported from the natural sciences to philosophy and influenced most thinking. Freud tried to apply it to the mind, a determination of the abstract.

PSYCHOLOGY

Psychology is a broad area and its basic ideas go back a long way. ASSOCIATION PSYCHOLOGY (the idea that ideas are connected to other ideas and forces) had been developed by thinkers like Berkeley, Hume and other philosophers. Psychology was interested in mental functioning but, influenced by positivism, tended to be experimental and determinist. Wiltham Wandt (1832 - 1920) published an important work PRINCIPLES OF PHYSIOLOGICAL PSYCHOLOGY in 1873. This stressed the importance of biological determinism and experiment.

PSYCHIATRY

Psychiatry is a newer science than psychology and developed rapidly in the late 19th Century. It was somewhat radical and interested in a new view of the mind. It considered certain illnesses that official medicine left out – like hysteria, lethargy, catalepsy. Psychiatry also thought about the origin of nervous illnesses, eventually coming up with the idea of mental energy. Emil Kraepilin (1856 - 1926) published a compendium (1883) synthesising modern psychiatry – talking about things like schizophrenia (although it wasn't called that then). He attempted to define mental illnesses scientifically .

13

The 19th century was dominated by advances in the natural sciences. Comte invented sociology, a positivist science of man, and Freud followed in that determinist and mechanist tradition.

Ernst Wilhelm von Brücke

Darwin

Theodor Meynert

19th century at a glance

Hegel

Herman von Helmholtz

Theodor Gomperz

J S Mill

Herman Nothnagel

Franz Brentano

16

17

I WAS ALWAYS AMBITIOUS, BUT CERTAIN THAT I WOULD SUCCEED, IN ONE WAY OR ANOTHER...

WHICH LED YOU INTO THIS · COCAINE DEAL?

YES OK, I DID THINK COCAINE WAS GOING TO BE THE ANSWER TO EVERYTHING, HOW WAS I TO KNOW EVERYONE WOULD GET ADDICTED, BUT AT LEAST IT'S GOOD FOR A LOCAL ANAESTHETIC.

YOUR FRIEND FLIESCHL - MARXOW ENDED UP ON HUGE AMOUNTS, ADDICTED AND DYING...

ALRIGHT, ALRIGHT, I KNOW I WAS TOO HASTY, TOO QUICK TO GENERALISE AND EAGER TO MAKE MY NAME, I LEARNT MY LESSON. NOW I AM VERY CAREFUL ALWAYS TO TEST HYPOTHESES CAREFULLY.

A REFORMED CHARACTER EH? THAT'S WHAT THEY ALL SAY.

OK, SO WHEN DID ALL THE HYSTERIA STUFF START?

THAT GOES BACK TO CHARCOT AND MY DEVELOPING INTEREST IN NEUROPATHOLOGY. THE WHOLE QUESTION OF HYSTERIA STARTED TO GET MORE AND MORE COMPLEX, I HAD NO IDEA WHERE IT WAS GOING

YOU'VE LOST ME, ALREADY.

THE FACT IS THAT LOCAL DIAGNOSIS AND ELECTRICAL REACTIONS LEAD NOWHERE IN THE STUDY OF HYSTERIA, WHEREAS A DETAILED DESCRIPTION OF MENTAL PROCESSES ENABLES ME TO OBTAIN AT LEAST SOME KIND OF INSIGHT INTO THE COURSE OF THAT AFFLICTION.

YOU CAN TRY AND BLIND ME WITH SCIENCE BUT I KNOW WHAT YOU'RE UP TO, YOU'RE TRYING TO CLAIM THAT THE OLD FASHIONED METHODS OF WATER TREATMENT AND ELECTRIC SHOCKS MIGHT GET THEM TO TALK BUT IT DOESN'T CURE THE DISEASE...

QUITE SO, IT MIGHT HAVE A TEMPORARY EFFECT BUT NOTHING MORE.

SO WHAT'S NEXT, IF IT AIN'T PHYSICAL, WHAT IS HYSTERIA, SOMETHING THAT DAMES GET WHEN THEY DON'T GET IT, IF YOU GET WHAT I MEAN?

YOUR VIEWS MAY BE COMMON BUT THEY ARE CERTAINLY WRONG IF NOT NEANDERTHAL. THIS IDEA THAT HYSTERIA IS A WOMAN'S DISEASE GOES RIGHT BACK TO THE GREEKS. AS YOU PROBABLY KNOW THE WORD MEANS "WOMB" IN GREEK.

GET OFF, YOU'RE HAVING ME ON! THEM GREEKS, THEY'RE TRICKY SO AND SO'S!

IT SIMPLY ILLUSTRATES WITH REMARKABLE FORCE THE HISTORICAL MYTHOLOGY WE ARE FACED WITH IN DEALING WITH HYSTERICAL SYMPTOMS. IF IT IS FELT TO BE SIMPLY A PHYSICAL REALITY OF THE FEMALE SPECIES, IT CAN BE ASCRIBED TO THEIR BIOLOGICAL INADEQUACIES THAT THEY SUFFER FROM HYSTERIA

AN' YOU'RE GONNA TELL ME IT AIN'T SO, WISE GUY.

COME WITH ME...

In 1885 Freud given a small travelling scholarship. With it he visited the famous neurologist, Charcot. Freud went to Paris to study with Charcot who was doing interesting work with hysterics. Basically Charcot had shown that hysterical symptoms weren't connected to anatomy. He had shown that hysterical patients could be hypnotised into making their symptoms disappear, or reappear.

Without realising it he had stumbled on something revolutionary. The real explanations of hysterical symptoms were not ultimately biological and mechanical.

Hysterics used to be burnt as witches or locked up and persecuted as possessed people. This was the common-sense approach. Although Charcot took a humane view of hysterics and thought they could be helped he also stuck to the view that hysteria was a form of hereditary degeneration. Charcot's demonstrations of patients under hypnosis fascinated Freud.

Charcot said that hypnosis could only be used on hysterics and that was because of their physical state. This kept the argument firmly in the mechanist camp and left Freud with a number of puzzles. He was convinced that hysteria was a real disease, not the product of malingering or demons, and that men as well as women suffered from it. Freud went back to Vienna full of these ideas about hypnotism, hysteria and cures, only to find that everyone ignored him.

Freud began to work with Josef Breuer, another physician who was interested in hysteria and who used hypnosis as a form of treatment. Breuer sent some patients to Freud and also helped him financially, as well as professionally. The result of their initial collaboration and analysis of patients was their book *Studies in Hysteria* (1895).

One of the most important things Freud and Breuer discovered was that the trigger for hysteria could itself be psychological. It was also noted that patients didn't remember the event. This was leading Freud towards the notion of unconscious memory processes and the idea of repression. It was confirmed time and again that once memory had been worked through, or brought into consciousness by hypnotism, then it

COULD IT BE JUST IDEAS?

disappeared. This could only be explained by considering how memories became repressed and distorted. The key breakthrough was the notion of REPRESSION (linked to sexuality).

The really difficult question was WHERE DID THIS RESISTANCE COME FROM? From his observation of patients Freud was increasingly led to believe that it derived from sexual desires or wishes that patients didn't want to admit. The fact that Breuer didn't want to go along with these conclusions, despite the evidence, seems to strengthen further the argument that resistance and repression are common features of the human mind. In 1886 Freud gave a lecture on male hysteria to the Vienna society of physicians outlining some of his ideas. The reaction was not promising and Freud thought it was positively hostile. Freud began to realise that he was plowing a lonely furrow and that the price of radical thinking might well be ridicule rather than fame.

Repressed sexuality was hardly likely to be a popular topic in an era when respectability was the keyword.

OUR WORK HAS BEEN VERY INTERESTING AND PRODUCTIVE, BUT I'M NOT SURE AS TO WHERE IT'S ALL LEADING...

LISTEN BREUER, WHICHEVER WAY I TURN THERE ARE PROBLEMS IN UNDERSTANDING NEUROTIC DISORDERS. I MUST FOLLOW IT THROUGH AND MAKE GREAT DISCOVERIES

SIGMUND, I MUST CONFESS THAT THIS PLUNGING INTO SEXUALITY IN THEORY AND PRACTICE IS NOT TO MY TASTE.

... BUT YOU KNOW AS WELL AS I, PARTICULARLY FROM THE ANNA O. CASE, THAT SEXUALITY IS EVERYTHING, IT IS THE ORIGIN OF DISORDER!?

HYPNOTISM AND A TALKING CURE HELPED, BUT THIS OBSESSION WITH SEXUALITY, IT IS JUST TOO MUCH.

BREUER, YOU HELD THE KEY IN YOUR HAND WITH ANNA O. AND YOU WILL NOT ENTER THE SECRET GARDEN...

I HAVE HELPED YOU IN MANY WAYS FREUD BUT I CANNOT GO FURTHER — YOU MUST RESOLVE THESE DIFFICULTIES YOURSELF.

I MUST GO TO WHERE THE TRUTH LIES... JUST BECAUSE IT IS BURIED AND YOU TOO REFUSE IT, THAT IS NOT REASON ENOUGH TO AVOID IT...

THE GREAT MAJORITY OF SEVERE NEUROSES IN WOMEN HAVE THEIR ORIGIN IN THE MARRIAGE BED

THERE IS SOMETHING ABOUT SEXUAL DRIVES THAT BUGS ME...

THE WAY IN WHICH SEXUAL EXPERIENCE IS REPRESSED MAKES IT HARD TO BRING INTO THE OPEN REPRESSION & RESISTANCE — AND UNCONSCIOUS MENTAL PROCESSES ARE REALITIES I MUST NOW BRING TO THE LIGHT OF DAY ...THOUGH I HAVE A STRONG FEELING THAT PEOPLE WILL NOT THANK ME FOR DOING IT...

WHY SYMPTOMS REAPPEAR CAN ONLY BE EXPLAINED BY UNDER- STANDING THE RETURN OF THE REPRESSED

MAYBE I CAN MAKE NEUROTICS JUST GENERALLY UNHAPPY, RATHER THAN MISERABLE..?

By 1887 Freud had a child, a few more patients and a new friend, one Wilhelm Fliess, an ear, nose and throat specialist from Berlin. Fliess came to Vienna to study and attended Freud's lectures on neurology.

In *The Interpretation of Dreams* Freud wrote "An intimate friend and a hated enemy have always been necessary requirements of my emotional life." Fliess was to be the intimate friend and enemies he found all over the place. For a man of genius Freud had pretty poor taste in friends. Even if we are nice about Wilhelm Fliess we'd have to say he was a weirdo. Perhaps he wasn't at the time Freud met him, but by the time he started writing books about how the world was based on rhythms of 23 and 28 and how the nose was a sexual organ he was getting there. He and Freud wrote to each other constantly. Actually Fliess also speculated about infantile sexuality well before Freud took over the idea.

Freud reported all of his thoughts and investigations to Fliess who played an important role as confidant, or sounding board. Only from Freud's letters to Fliess do we know of the advances that Freud was making in his theoretical work. Fliess read and commented on all his work, being a useful editor and critic. They had what they called little "congresses" sometimes up mountains and sometimes in Berlin. It was in a letter to Fliess that Freud wrote, "A man like me cannot live without a hobby horse, without a dominating passion, without a tyrant, and he has come my way. And in his service I now know no moderation. It is psychology."

The strange influence of Fliess can be seen in The Seduction theory drama. Freud had come to the conclusion that all neuroses were the result of real sexual abuse in childhood, mostly by the father.

This view was applauded by Fliess and Freud himself seemed to think it was a satisfactory explanation of many complex factors. This Seduction theory scandal has not really gone away ever since, and Freud surely regretted his precipitate acceptance of the idea.

Freud decided to say in print that he had discovered the origin of neurotic behaviour and in fact gave a famous lecture to the local Society for Psychiatry and Neurology in which he committed himself to the Seduction Theory. This may well have been something of an error of judgement on Freud's part. He told the assembled audience that he had discovered the source of the Nile, the solution to a thousand year old problem but they weren't very impressed. "The lecture had an icy reception from the donkeys" Freud wrote, which was just a little arrogant since he later abandoned the theory. Krafft-Ebing, the renowned sexual theorist, said that it sounded like a scientific fairy-tale. The idea that all neuroses came from sexual abuse of one kind or another in early life really was a little odd since it seemed to suggest that almost all fathers were potential, if not actual, abusers. Not surprisingly Freud gave up the idea altogether in 1897 and said that the idea had broken down under its own improbability. It was back to the drawing board for psychoanalysis.

One of the turning points in the development of psychoanalysis was the death of Freud's father in October 1896. It turned Freud in on himself and led his thinking in a new direction. He later said that his reaction to his father's death showed that it was the most significant, the most decisive loss, of a man's life.

This emphasis on the male, and on the father, many people argue, coloured Freud's whole approach.

Freud felt completely uprooted, and even guilty. He was experiencing what he later called the 'return of the repressed'. His feelings about his father which he had repressed, feelings such as rivalry, jealousy, ambition and resentment returned to him as remorse, shame, impotence and inhibition. His mind was full of feelings from an earlier period, he was battling with the ghosts of the past. His self-analysis consisted of calmly looking at these phantoms and assessing how they affected him. Self-analysis turned to memories of childhood.

Freud was already working on dream analysis and he began to realise that more and more frequently the unconscious wish in the dream came from childhood memories. From this analysis Freud came to the conclusion that the unconscious of an adult is very much created by the child who lies within. The love for the mother, the competition with the father, the fear of castration, the resolution of these feelings in coming to adulthood and their continuing effects in dreams and the unconscious, all of these things came to Freud through his intensive self-analysis from 1896-99. In this process Freud employed the free association technique which was to become the hallmark of psychoanalysis. He abandoned hypnotism after his self-analysis and in fact relied on his dreams as the main material on which he worked. Having realised that his patients suffered from resistance, Freud wasn't entirely surprised that he also did during this period and at times progress was slow and difficult. In the last phase of the this epochal self-analysis Freud began to write the *Interpretation of Dreams*. It was as if a new Freud, a new theory and a new science, psychoanalysis, were all born in this struggle for self-elucidation.

The child's secret passion for the mother, which cannot remain innocent, gets connected up with sexual development. The inevitable fear of the father as a rival leads to the famous Oedipus complex.

Dr Freud, neuropathologist, father and not very succesful practitioner, very unpopular with the Viennese and uncertain of his methodology went into self-analysis. He reappears as Sigmund Freud, father of psychoanalysis, certain of his discoveries, author of the *Interpretation of Dreams,* which sums up all his major ideas and confident of what, how and in which manner he should treat his patients. It had been quite a long and complicated road from searching for the gonads of eels to mining the hidden treasures of the unconscious, but Freud had stuck to it tenaciously. From Charcot's thinking about hysteria to Breuer's worrying about patients' love for their doctors, Sigmund had always concentrated on trying to explain why people acted in a manner that seemed irrational but actually reflected some real problem for them. He had been discovering the laws of the unconscious, a world that had only been glimpsed at before.

The mystery of the human soul, Freud argued, lay in the pyschic dramas of their childhood. Unravel that and a cure seemed certain. Eureka! (1900)

To try and reconstruct where Freud had got to, we need to back track a little and look at some famous cases, like Anna O. But we need also to look at one other thing.

In 1895 Freud had written an extremely ambitious paper called a *Project for a Scientific Psychology* in which he planned "to investigate what form the theory of mental functioning assumes if one introduces the quantitive point of view , a sort of economics of nerve forces." This was the sort of determinist thinking that pops up everywhere and shows Freud trying to describe the whole mental machinery as a kind of apparatus that could be analysed like a hydraulic system. Freud keeps talking about the laws of the mind as if they were indeed somewhat akin to the laws of physics. Drives and energy, the primary and secondary processes, neurons and particles, it all sounds more like chemistry than systems of ideas.

As if this whole natural-scientific psychology wasn't enough Freud also announced in the paper that he was looking to "extract from psychopathology a gain for normal psychology." That is he wanted to rewrite everything already known about the ordinary functions of the mind in the light of what he was discovering from the abnormal. Vastly ambitious and overwhelmingly all-inclusive, that was all.

35

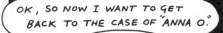

OK, SO NOW I WANT TO GET BACK TO THE CASE OF "ANNA O."

WHAT?

SPILL THE BEANS SIGI — WHAT'S THE TRUTH ON THIS GAL?

SHE WAS A PATIENT OF BREUER'S WITH SEVERE HYSTERIA SYMPTOMS. SHE FELL IN LOVE WITH HIM, AND, I BELIEVE, HE WITH HER..

THE USUAL STORY EH, DOC?

NOT AT ALL — SHE SIMPLY RE-INVENTED HYPNOTISM, ADAPTING IT TO HER ILLNESS

NOW THAT SOUNDS LIKE A LEADING STATEMENT.. TO ME...

IN SOME WAYS SHE WAS AHEAD OF BREUER, SHE WAS VERY INTELLIGENT AND SHE CALLED HER WAY OF DEALING WITH HER SYMPTOMS "MY TALKING CURE", AND "CHIMNEY SWEEPING"

KEEP TALKING...

WELL, WE WERE TRYING TO WORK OUT WHAT WAS GOING ON, LOOKING FOR CLUES...

LIKE, WHY SHE SAID SHE WAS HAVING HIS BABY...

HOW DID YOU KNOW ABOUT THAT?

EASY, SIGI — — SHE TOLD ME...

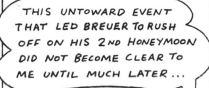

THIS UNTOWARD EVENT THAT LED BREUER TO RUSH OFF ON HIS 2ND HONEYMOON DID NOT BECOME CLEAR TO ME UNTIL MUCH LATER...

IT'S CLEAR AS BOURBON TO ME, DID SHE HAVE HIS BABY OR NOT..?

.. OF COURSE NOT — BUT SHE IMAGINED SHE DID IN HER UNCONSCIOUS — DON'T YOU SEE, THE HYSTERICAL SYMPTOMS WERE IMAGINARY ....

THIS I DON'T GET, HOW CAN IDEAS CAUSE ILLNESS, HOW CAN YOU THINK SOMETHING YOU DON'T KNOW YOU'RE THINKING ..?

THIS IS WHERE THE KEY TERM REPRESSION COMES IN ...

I'M TALKING TOO MUCH — TELL ME AGAIN — WHAT'S THIS UNCONSCIOUS IDEA, AND WHAT'S "ANNA O." GOT TO DO WITH IT ALL ..?

IF YOU CONSIDER HOW "ANNA O"'S SYMPTOMS CAME AND WENT, THEY ALL DERIVED FROM REPRESSION.

INSTITUTE FOR SOCIAL WORK

I TRACKED HER DOWN — REAL NAME'S BERTHA PAPPENHEIM..

INSIDE—

AH, DR. FREUD! I REMEMBER YOU WELL, AS I DO DR. BREUER

...YOU ARE RECOVERED THEN FROM YOUR NERVOUS AFFLICTION, RELATED AS I RECALL TO YOUR FATHER'S FATAL ILLNESS?

I WAS IN AN INSTITUTION FOR A TIME, BUT NOW I AM WELL — HARD WORKING AND DEDICATED TO MY SOCIAL WORK

SO "ANNA", WHAT REALLY HAPPENED?

AS I EXPLAINED TO BREUER MY "NAUGHTY STATES" COULD BE CLEARED BY A SORT OF HYPNOSIS — I WOULD GO INTO A TRANCE AND WOULD LATER AWAKEN FEELING CLEAR AND MENTALLY NORMAL..

YOU TALKED TO BREUER A LOT ABOUT YOUR SYMPTOMS — EVERY DAY IN FACT?

I DISCOVERED THAT IF I DESCRIBED THE ONSET OF A SYMPTOM IT THEN CLEARED UP, BREUER WAS REALLY FASCINATED BY THIS, AND I THINK, BY ME ...

NOW, THIS IS WHERE I DISCOVERED "TRANSFERENCE" AND "COUNTER-TRANSFERENCE" YOU KNOW...

Mainly through the insights generated by Anna O, Freud was more and more attracted by the talking out cure. Hypnosis seemed to cure things but often the problem returned, even if in a different form. All this led Freud to the idea that the neurotic problems were more rooted than first appeared.

Free Association led to a deeper and deeper probing into the mind of his patients.

When Freud began to understand that these forces were ucs, this was the turning point in his scientific life. He put aside physiology and neurology and became a psychological detective.

Therapy, self-analysis and talking out lead to models of the mind and to a notion of universal psychic patterns.

With the publication of the *Interpretation of Dreams*, Freud consolidated all of his previous work.

In it Freud says, "the interpretation of dreams is in fact the Royal road to a knowledge of the unconscious; it is the securest foundation of psychoanalysis."

Through his use of the analytic session with free association now the only and indispensable rule, combined with the analysis of dreams, Freud set out all the major foundations of psychoanalysis.

Free association was vital because getting back to earlier memories was constantly blocked by resistance and transference. Hypnosis and the pressure technique weren't adequate because neither could deal with resistance and repression, only free association could lead to the hidden connection between ideas and images. You can't force patients to make things conscious – you can only tickle out the things that are swimming in the unconscious by careful analysis of the fragments on the surface – the free association.

The Interpretation of Dreams sets out to do two things; to demonstrate how his theories of the unconscious mind are confirmed through dream analysis and to demonstrate how dream analysis works.

He says that all dreams are meaningful,

- that each dream has a cause

- that we only remember the manifest content of the dream (what happens in the dream)

- that the latent (or repressed and unconscious part) is the cause of a dream.

- there is a complex relationship between the two which can only be exposed through free association.

Let us look in more detail at what Freud says about dreams and the consequences of his interpretation.

BELLE VUE

IN THIS HOUSE ON 24ᵀᴴ JULY 1895

THE SECRET OF DREAMS WAS REVEALED

TO DOCTOR SIGMUND FREUD

Freud argued that "All dreams are wish-fulfilment".

WAKE UP, DOC, I NEED TO ASK YOU A FEW QUESTIONS

I HAD THIS TERRIBLE DREAM LAST NIGHT — I WAS A WOMAN WITH 6 KIDS AND SOMEONE ON AN ELEPHANT KEPT ON EATING THEM — WHAT DOES IT MEAN?

* You should bear in mind that the dreams which we produce at night have, on the one hand, the greatest external similarity and internal kinship with the creations of insanity, and are, on the other hand, compatible with complete health in waking life.

DREAMS →

SO?

* Dreams have been subjected to distortion; the psychical process underlying them might originally have been expressed in words quite differently. You must distinguish the *manifest content of the dream*, as you vaguely recollect it in the morning and laboriously (and, as it seems, abitrarily) clothe it in words, and the *latent dream-thoughts*, which you must suppose were present in the unconscious. This distortion in dreams is the same process that you have already come to know in investigating the formation of hysterical symptoms.

* You can also obtain a view, by a synthetic work, of the process which has brought about the distortion of the unconscious dream-thoughts into the manifest content of the dream. We call this process the 'dream-work', It deserves our closest theoretical interest, since we are able to study in it, as nowhere else, what unsuspected psychical processes can occur in the unconscious, or rather, to put it more accurately, *between* two separate psychical systems like the conscious and unconscious.

* Among these freshly discovered psychical processes those of *condensation* and *displacement* are especially noteable. The dream-work is a special case of the effects produced by two different mental groupings on each other – that is, of the consequences of mental splitting; and it seems identical in all essentials with the process of distortion which transforms the repressed complexes into symptoms where there is unsuccessful repression.

* You will also learn with astonishment from the analysis of dreams (and most convincingly from that of your own) what an unsuspectedly great part is played in human development by impressions and experiences of early childhood. In dream-life the child that is in man pursues its existence, as it were, and retains all its characteristics and wishful impulses, even such as have become unserviceable in later life. There will be brought home to you with irresistible force the many developments, repressions, sublimations and reaction-formations, by means of which a child with a quite other innate endowment grows into what we call a normal man, the bearer, and in part the victim, of the civilization that has been so painfully acquired.

* This is all from the *Interpretation of Dreams*.

45

The Origin of Dreams

The obvious question is where do dreams come from, what causes a particular dream. Freud says some of the main information in dreams derives from:

1) Recent events and obvious emotional facts like being made angry. Revenge is obtained in the dream – simple wish-fulfilment.

2) Many ideas are blended together by the dream – otherwise known as 'condensation".

3) 'Displacement', an important event may be represented by a recent but unimportant memory. Free association uncovers the links.

4) Long buried memories are represented by recent trivial ideas. Deep displacement which only psychoanalysis can uncover.

Here's an example Freud gave of a dream that initially didn't seem to fit the bill.

47

How dreams work – one of Freud's classic dream analyses

The Dream Machine

Freud thereby discovers that the hidden wish in dreams is often in adults of a sexual nature.

Also, and importantly, that repressed thoughts still have to get past censorship before they can enter the strange world of dreams.

That in analysing dreams the similarity between the neurotic and the normal is made more apparent.

That the function of dreams is to discharge the tensions of repressed and forbidden wishes.

That the universitality of the unconscious is demonstrated by the workings of repression in dreams.

That the mechanisms of the dream work are

1) Condensation

That one image can stand for many associations. The complexity of the latent content of a dream can therefore be derived from analysing how repressed ideas, old ideas, unrecognised ideas and unthought out associations connect

up with the condensed image that is at the forefront of the dream. The way that a single idea, or event can simultaneously represent different impulses, Freud calls 'over-determination'.

2) Displacement

This is where the feelings related to one thing are connected to a different one, thus for example the murderous feelings about the sister-in-law are displaced unto the little white dog in the example before.

3) Dramatisation

Interestingly dreams are of course almost wholly visual, rather like a film. Like some bad films there often seems to be little connection between the events and images in a dream. However, as they say, every picture tells a story. In dreams, the story is hidden and the visuals are the clue.

4) Symbolisation

Images stand in for, symbolise, other things. Phallic symbols are now widely recognised (interestingly), such as guns, tall round buildings etc. Dreams make great use of symbols. Freud said 'in dreams symbols are used almost exclusively for the expression of sexual objects and relations'.

5) Secondary Elaboration

When someone wakes up they recall their dream and start to think about what it means. This starts with an interpretation which can take you further away from the latent content.

So in all we can say that dreams are distorted, disguised versions of hidden and repressed wishes. They are what the conscious mind gets as a report of what is going on in the unconscious, only through a scrambler.

If Freud is right about dreams, and he surely is, then the *Interpretation of Dreams* is conclusive evidence of the existence of the unconscious. What else this proves is more difficult to analyse.

The way in which Freud understood the role of symbols in dreams, their ability to carry other meanings, profoundly affect our understanding of modern culture.

Television advertising is simply symbols in action or psychoanalysis put into practise.

ALL DREAMS, WITHOUT EXCEPTION, ARE WISH FULFILMENT — RIGHT SIGGIE?

YES DARLINK, BUT WHAT ABOUT STRAIGHT FORWARD ZINGS LIKE IF YOU'RE ZIRSTY SO YOU DREAM OF A DRINK?

DREAMS ARE PRIMARILY CONCERNED WITH INFANTILE-SEXUALITY, THE INDESPENSABLE ORGANIC FOUNDATION OF PSYCHIC ANALYSIS ...

WHAT DO YOU MEAN?

ZIS SORT OF DREAM DOESN'T TAKE YOU BACK TO CHILDHOOD AT ALL — JUST TO BEING ZIRSTY

HUMPH!

... ZEN ZERE ARE ZE DREAMS OF WAR, TRAUMATIC DREAMS — ZIS IS NOT WISH FULFILMENT BUT NIGHTMARE!

WELL — YES, BUT...

THIS MAY BE THAT THE DREAM-WORK HAS FAILED.

... AND MY DEAR, ALL OF ZE ANXIETY ONES AS WELL ..

AND ZEN, ZERE ARE ZE REALLY DIRTY DREAMS, WITH NO CENSORSHIP AT ALL — JUST GOOD CLEAN FILTH!

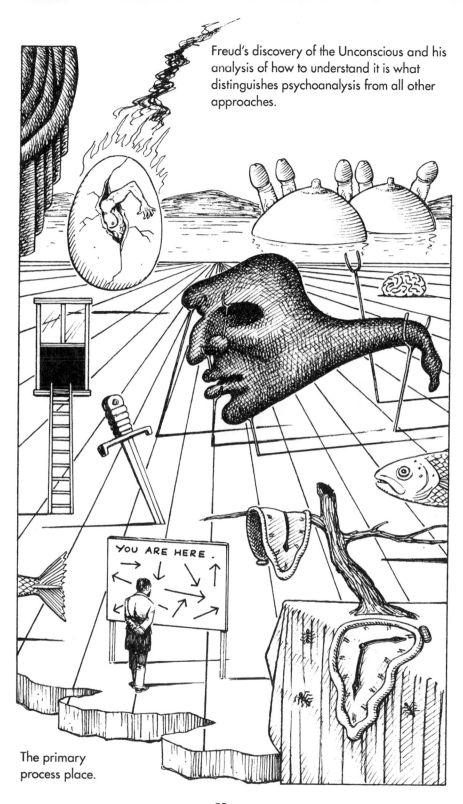

Freud's discovery of the Unconscious and his analysis of how to understand it is what distinguishes psychoanalysis from all other approaches.

YOU ARE HERE.

The primary process place.

Freud's discovery of the Unconscious and of its importance in psychic life is the very bedrock of psychoanalysis. Through self-analysis and the Interpretation of Dreams, and then other everyday symptoms, Freud came to his theories of infantile sexuality, the stages of development and an understanding of the power of the unconscious. The difficulties of developing these theories may, in part, explain Freud's insistence on their inviolability. The laws of the Unconscious became the Commandments of the Psychoanalysis Society.

But what is the Unconscious?

THE UNCONSCIOUS RULES OK

The term 'unconscious' is used by Freud in a number of different senses. It is used in a purely *descriptive* sense to suggest all those contents which are not present to consciousness. This is the common sense notion of the Unconscious. The first technical use of the term by Freud is the notion of the unconscious in the *dynamic* sense. This refers, not to any particular quality of a mental state, but to its function. That is to say the unconscious is the site of repressed forces struggling to break into consciousness, but they are held in check by a repressing agency. This dynamic view led in turn to a *systematic* or structural view in which the psychical apparatus is seen as consisting of a number of different regions or agencies each responsible for different functions. This culminates in the 1914 paper, *The Unconscious*, in the meta psychological view of the psychical apparatus which is made up of the following elements:

THE UNCONSCIOUS ISN'T A PLACE, A THING, IT'S THAT PART OF THE MIND THAT IS REPRESSED.

1. The *dynamic* point of view – which sees the mind as the site of an interplay of opposing forces and to which the mechanism of repression is crucial.

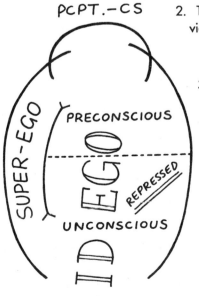

PCPT.–CS

SUPER-EGO

PRECONSCIOUS

EGO

REPRESSED

[I]

UNCONSCIOUS

ID

2. The *topographic* or systematic point of view which sees the mind divided into various systems with different functions and characteristics.

3. The *economic* point of view which 'endeavours to follow out the vicissitudes of amounts of excitation and to arrive at some relative estimate of their magnitude'.

In this 1914 paper Freud also presents in detail what is known as the 'first topography'. According to this view, the mind consists of three systems: the unconscious proper (Ucs), the preconscious (Pcs), and the consciousness-perception system (Cs). The system Ucs, contains those contents which have been repressed either by the process of *primal repression* or *after-repression*. The system Pcs contains those contents which, while not being conscious, are capable of becoming conscious, ie, are not repressed. The Cs contains all those contents which are conscious in the descriptive sense.

Repression takes place on the border between the system Ucs and Pcs (Cs). It is a dynamic concept, ie, it can only be understood in terms of conceiving the psychical apparatus as a system of forces which necessarily enter into conflict with each other, this psychical conflict having its ultimate basis in instinctual dualism. However, in describing the mechanism of repression, it is necessary to employ the economic notion of cathexis. This is the notion of a definite quantity of psychical energy which becomes attached to an idea or a group of ideas. In after-repression (recession proper), the repression takes place from two directions simultaneously. Cathexis is withdrawn from the idea in the Pcs, and it either retains its Ucs cathexis or gains a new Ucs cathexis. So in the case of after-repression, there is both a repulsion of the idea from the Pcs, and an attraction of it into the Ucs. But there is a difficulty here in accounting for why, when the cathexis has been withdrawn from the idea in Pcs, the cathected Ucs content does not force itself through the censorship again. For this reason, and also to account for primal repression, it is necessary to postulate a further process: that of an *anticathexis* deriving from Pcs. This is a force of psychical energy which continues to hold the undesirable idea under repression in Ucs.

HEY SIGGIE, I KEEP ASKIN' YA TO MAKE IT SIMPLE FOR BEGINNERS..

JESUS, WHY COULDN'T YOU JUST SAY THAT INSTEAD OF ALL THAT STUFF ABOUT CATHEXIS & SYSTEMS?

HA HA!

OH HO HO!

WELL, ROUGHLY SPEAKING, THERE'S THE PLEASURE PRINCIPLE & THE REALITY PRINCIPLE. THE PRIMARY PROCESS IS ABOUT PLEASURE AND THE SECONDARY IS ABOUT REALITY

THE UNCONSCIOUS FOLLOWS THE PLEASURE PRINCIPLE, IT WANTS TO SATISFY INSTINCTS AND DESIRES; IT IS LIKE A DREAM WORLD FULL OF STRANGE EMOTIONS

.. AND THE REALITY PRINCIPLE STOPS THEM DESIRES POPPIN' OUT, PUTS A LID ON 'EM AND SAYS HEY, WE NEED SOME ORDER AROUND HERE ...

THAT'S JUST WHAT I SAID ☼

CUSTARD

SPLAT!

IF YOU WILL, YES, BUT THE REALITY PRINCIPLE MODIFIES THE PLEASURE PRINCIPLE AND ALSO GOVERNS THE LIFE OF THE INSTINCTS

For Freud instinctual drives are basic in shaping a person's life. These instinctual drives are ever present, a power that can explode, or be directed in many ways. The sexual instinct is the most important, what Freud called the libido.

Basically Freud says that the manner in which an individual channels their libido, or is driven by it, determines their character. The damming up of libido can produce hysteria, anxiety, or explosive eruptions of psychic disorder.

Instincts will pop up later as a major problem.

Psychopathology of Everyday Life

After the great work *Interpretation of Dreams* Freud set out to show that psychoanalysis wasn't just a theory about abnormality but a description of how the human mind in general worked. In his book *The Psycho-Pathology of Everyday Life* Freud wanted to show that the unconscious operated in and through what we describe as everyday events, such as slips of the tongue, errors, omissions, faulty memories, etc. The basic point was that none of these occurrences were actually innocent as far as Freud was concerned, they revealed stratagems of the unconscious mind.

"*Bungled actions*, like other errors, are often used to fulfil wishes which one ought to deny oneself. Here the intention disguises itself as a lucky accident. For instance, as happened to one of my friends, a man may be due, obviously against his will, to go by train to visit someone near the town where he lives, and then, at a junction where he has to change, may by mistake get into a train that takes him back to where he came from. Or someone on a journey may be anxious to make a stop at an intermediate station but may be forbidden from doing so by other obligations, and he may then overlook or miss some connection so that he is obliged to break his journey in the way he wished. Or what happened to one of my patients: I had forbidden him to telephone the girl he was in love with, and then, when he meant to telephone me, he asked for the wrong number 'by mistake' or 'while he was thinking of something else' and suddenly found himself connected to the girl's number..."

Jokes and their relation to the Unconscious

Freud collected jokes, mainly Jewish jokes and he talked about wit and the unconscious in the *Interpretation of Dreams*. He pointed out that the repression and sublimation of unconscious processes was intimately related to the theory of the joke and the comic. Funnily enough his book about it all *Jokes and their Relation to the Unconscious* was about as witty as a wet Wednesday.

(How does a psychoanalyst get his mother on the couch? Charges her half price for an introductory session.) This is an example of what Freud called a tendentious joke by which he meant the indirect expression of hostility or obscenity. (This is also a cheap joke.) Innocent jokes depend upon verbal ingenuity. (See p.   (Eysenck)) Also for example, "he's too Jung to be a Freudian?."

In his wonderfully methodical way Freud analyses the technique of jokes and comes to the conclusion that they are like neurotic symptoms, dreams and slips of the tongue. In line with his model of the mechanical instincts at work Freud talks about the function of jokes, particularly tendentious jokes, as being one of releasing an inhibition. After some interminable analysis Freud says,

And here at last we can understand what it is that jokes achieve in the service of their purpose. They make possible the satisfaction of an instinct (whether lustful or hostile) in the face of an obstacle that stands in its way. They circumvent this obstacle and in that way draw pleasure from a source which the obstacle had made inaccessible.

Freud then goes on to try to show that all jokes conform to a pattern that he can then express as a kind of instinctual formula, a sort of barometer of jokiness. He claims that the yield of pleasure corresponds to the psychical expenditure that is saved in condensing or economising on the expenditure of psychic energy.

Freud then goes on to try to show that all jokes conform to a pattern that he can then express as a kind of instinctual formula, a sort of barometer of jokiness. He claims that the yield of pleasure corresponds to the psychical expenditure that is saved in condensing or economising on the expenditure of psychic energy.

So that playing with words is rather like fore-play, or minor sexual gratification. (I thought fore-play was a two couple orgy that didn't get anywhere.)

Insofar as Freud had a sense of humour it was of the rather gloomy kind like, "The only trouble with operations on my jaw is that you have to stop smoking for two hours." Really funny jokes Freud put into the manic state analysis as being the discharge of massively surplus instinctual energy at a rate incommensurate with the everyday. In fact Freud's analysis of jokes shows him at his worst, the tendency to reduce everything to sexual mechanics, a reductionism in relation to the form of things and a desire to explain everything within one set of rules. Having divided jokes up into innocent and tendentious Freud later drops the innocent bit and says that ultimately they are "in fact never non-tendentious".

This means that in the end all kinds of jokes really are simply a technique for delivering a kind of repressed sensual gratification.

This approach is limited in that it ignores the pleasure of the verbal ingenuity of jokes, their expression of aggression, their mocking of power, their politics, the complexity of word games, the silliness of jokes, the surreal, the cathartic release, etc. etc. A good joke is like psycho-analysis in reverse but speeded up and set to music. So humour is probably indicative of psychic health and humanity, not the simple functioning of a mental machine in disequilibrium. (Although the one doesn't exclude the other.)

What did Oedipus say to his father at the crossroads?

"I've got the mother of all headaches".

Back to the
couch as Freud
used to say.

After everyday life, which consists
of mistakes, bad food, indigestion, dissension
and disagreements, as well as weird patients
and wars, it's time to get back to the problem
of neurotics. There are always people
with severe illnesses.

We need to examine:

1) Hysteria (and what it is)

2) Anxiety and its causes

3) Obsessional disorders (next page)

4) Depression and neuroses.

5) Paranoid personalities

6) Sexual immaturity and regression.

And note that:

All psychic conflict appears to come from the opposition between self-preservation and the sexual drive. Or we can say the reality principle and the Pleasure principle. Repression is the foundation of the theory of the unconscious. The dynamics of repression are the business of psychoanalysis. The energy in the system comes from the drives.

In all of Freud's work he recognised the reality of neuroses and their debilitating effects on patients. The work on dreams, slips of the tongue, primary and secondary processes were all concerned with the way in which the ego defended itself against ideas that were too painful, that had been repressed. It was in his work on obsessional neurosis that the importance of childhood sexuality began to emerge more clearly. Obsessional ideas, Freud said, are invariably self-reproaches which have re-emerged from repression in a changed form and which always relate to some sexual act in childhood. In fact Freud had a patient who was obsessed about killing somebody and wouldn't go out in case he did. In analysis Freud discovered that this patient constantly made up alibis in case someone did accuse him of murder. Freud worked out that the alibi was a classic defence mechanism related to the long repressed desire to kill his own father, who was a threat to him since he loved and desired his mother. This was the return of the repressed.

".. AND NOW FOR SOMETHING COMPLETELY DIFFERENT — SEX! (AND INFANTS)"

"... AND I SAID TO HUBBY, THE POINT IS THAT THE SEXUAL DRIVE AND THE SEXUAL OBJECT ARE DIFFERENT THINGS.."

"THE BLOODY TROUBLE WITH THAT IN INFANTS IS THAT THEY DEVELOP FROM POLYMORPHOUSLY PERVERSE INFANTS TO ADULTS AND THE PROCESS CAN GO WRONG — THEY CAN END UP IN LOVE WITH A BLOODY BOAT."

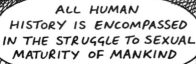

"WELL, WITH YOUR HUBBY THEY MIGHT BE."

"THE DEVELOPMENT OF THE SEXUAL DRIVE IN INFANTS MAPS OUT THEIR PSYCHO-SEXUAL HISTORY AS AN ADULT. I GOT STUCK."

"ALL HUMAN HISTORY IS ENCOMPASSED IN THE STRUGGLE TO SEXUAL MATURITY OF MANKIND"

"CUP OF TEA DEAR AND YES THE REASON PSYCHO ANALYSIS IS A PROBLEM IS THAT IT'S HARD TO UNDERSTAND AND HARD TO TOLERATE.."

"WHAT DID SIGMUND SAY ABOUT INFANT SEXUALITY, DEAR?"

"OH, SOMETHING ABOUT PHASES, TWO LUMPS OR THREE?"

THE FREUDIAN SUBJECT

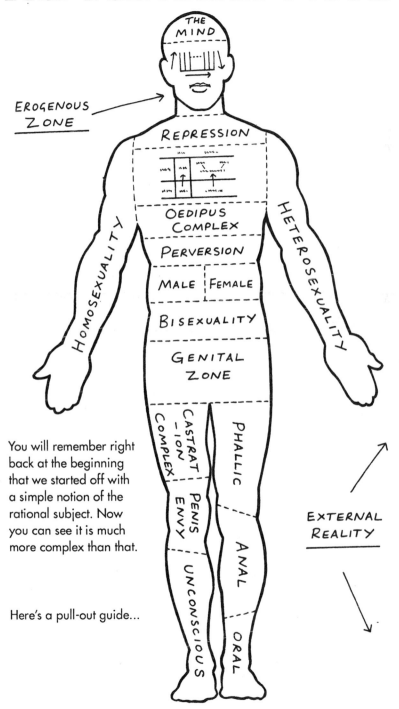

THE MIND

EROGENOUS ZONE

REPRESSION

OEDIPUS COMPLEX

PERVERSION

MALE | FEMALE

BISEXUALITY

GENITAL ZONE

HOMOSEXUALITY

HETEROSEXUALITY

CASTRATION COMPLEX

PENIS ENVY

PHALLIC

ANAL

ORAL

UNCONSCIOUS

EXTERNAL REALITY

You will remember right back at the beginning that we started off with a simple notion of the rational subject. Now you can see it is much more complex than that.

Here's a pull-out guide...

Three Essays on Sexuality (1905)

Freud completely overturned conventional notions of what is sexually normal.

As Freud himself said,

"According to the prevailing view, human sexual life consists essentially in an endeavour to bring one's own genitals into contact with those of someone of the opposite sex. With this are associated, as accessory phenomena and introductory acts, kissing this extraneous body, looking at it and touching it. This endeavour is supposed to make its appearance at puberty – that is, at the age of sexual maturity – and to serve the purposes of reproduction. Nevertheless, certain facts have always been known which do not fit into the narrow framework of this view.

1. It is a remarkable fact that there are people who are only attracted by individuals of their own sex and by their genitals.

2. It is equally remarkable that there are people whose desires behave exactly like sexual ones but who at the same time entirely disregard the sexual organs or their normal use; people of this kind are known as 'perverts'.

3. And lastly it is a striking thing that some children (who are on that account regarded as degenerate) take a very early interest in their genitals and show signs of excitation in them.

The point is that the sexual drive and the object it attaches too can be very different.

It may well be believed that psychoanalysis provoked astonishment and denials when, partly on the basis of these three neglected facts, it contradicted all the popular opinions on sexuality. Its principal findings are as follows:

a) Sexual life does not begin only at puberty, but starts with plain manifestations soon after birth.

b) It is necessary to distinguish sharply between the concepts of 'sexual' and 'genital'. The former is the wider concept and includes many activities that have nothing to do with the genitals.

c) Sexual life includes the function of obtaining pleasure from zones of the body – a function which is subsequently brought into the service of reproduction. The two functions often fail to coincide completely.

The chief interest is naturally focused on the first of these assertions, the most unexpected of all. It has been found that in early childhood there are signs of bodily activity to which only an ancient prejudice could deny the name of sexual and which are linked to psychical phenomena that we come across later in adult erotic life – such as fixation to particular objects, jealousy, and so on. It is further found, however, that these phenomena which emerge in early childhood form part of an ordered course of development, that they pass through a regular process of increase, reaching a climax towards the end of the fifth year, after which there follows a lull. During this lull progress is at a standstill and much is unlearnt and there is much recession.

(This is the man himself talking)

Sigmund then says,

"After the end of this period of latency, as it is called, sexual life advances once more with puberty; we might say that it has a second efflorescence. And here we come upon the fact that the onset of sexual life is diphasic, that it occurs in two waves – something that is unknown except in man and evidently has an important bearing on hominization. It is not a matter of indifference that the events of this early period, except for a few residues, fall a victim to *infantile amnesia*. Our views on the aetiology of the neuroses and our technique of analytical therapy are derived from these misconceptions; and our tracing of the developmental processes in this early period has also provided evidence for yet other conclusions.

The first organ to emerge as an erotogenic zone and to make libidinal demands on the mind is, from the time of birth onwards, the mouth. To begin with, all psychical activity is concentrated on providing satisfaction for the needs of that zone. Primarily, of course, this satisfaction serves the purpose of self-preservation by means of nourishment; but physiology should not be confused with psychology. The baby's obstinate persistence in sucking gives evidence at an early stage of a need for satisfaction which, though it originates from and is instigated by the taking of nourishment, nevertheless strives to obtain pleasure independently of nourishment and for that reason may and should be termed *sexual*."

We'll run through that again to try and establish how infantile sexuality shapes the contours of the mind in adult life.

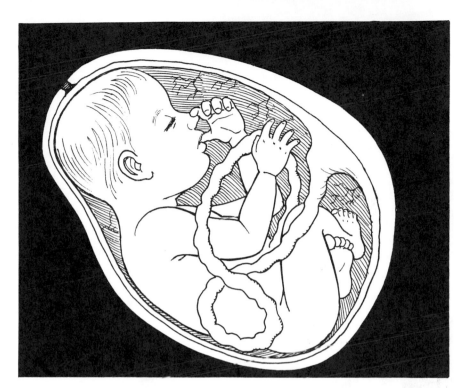

Freud's work is about how the biological human animal becomes a social and human subject. He initially had a strict chronology of the phases of development.

From the bliss of the womb the infant is suddenly thrown into the trauma of a terrifying world. How it finds itself as social subject is what it is all about.

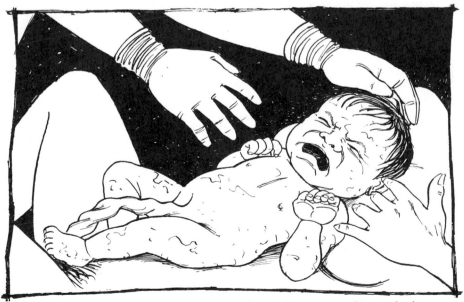

How the sexual drive gets adapted by the individual is what we can call its psycho-history.

73

The Oral Phase

In this development the early phase centres around the mouth. It is important to see how this erotogenic zone becomes established. First of all it is bound up with a vital somatic function, that is feeding.

Then there is a pleasurable sensation associated with the zone. Next comes the need to repeat the sensation, or desire. Sucking at the mother's breast is the starting point of the whole sexual life. The breast is the first love object.

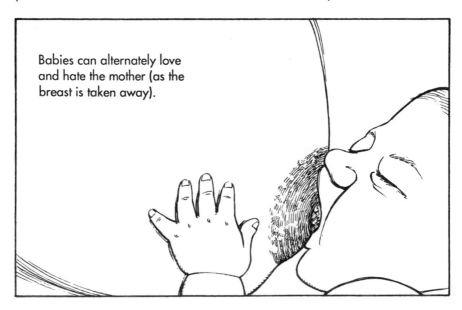

Babies can alternately love and hate the mother (as the breast is taken away).

THE ORAL PHASE CAN BE VERY IMPORTANT ...

These early pleasures can linger in many ways. Thumb sucking, Freud thought, was an example of the most simple and primitive infantile sexual activity. Thumb sucking is also an example of regressive behaviour, a return to an erotogenic zone. In fact the first organ to emerge as an erotogenic zone and to make libidinal demands on the mind is the mouth. The need to suck at the breast is replaced by a desire to obtain pleasure from so doing. Feeding becomes fun and is turned into what would loosely be called a sexual, or sensuous activity. Eating disorders clearly relate back to these earlier activities and oral pleasure is an important part of gourmet delight, smoking and drinking.

Freud didn't take much notice of the oral phase at all though. It was the post-Freudian who returned to look at the pre-Oedipal period.

The second erotogenic zone, or second phase, is the anal. The most simple anal pleasure is of emptying the bowels, 'doing a number 2' as the scientists say. The child can either gain satisfaction from performing for the parents, giving them a gift or can withhold and defy them. This withholding can become a fixation, an anal type character, and the connection between money and faeces has often been noticed. Overall holding it in or giving it out gets mixed up with feelings about mummy and daddy and if the whole business isn't handled properly people get stuck in this anal mode. (The expression 'tight-arsed' is psychoanalytically precise in describing mean people.)

Parental disapproval of the child's interest in faeces can also lead to intense repression and an obsession with filth and dirtiness. Horror at the body's function, of uncleanliness, can spill over into all sorts of cultural forms in adult life.

Then comes the Phallic phase

Freud actually didn't talk about this phase until quite late (1923). Children get into it fairly early.

This is the phase in which the child comes to be aware of its genital zone, moving on from the oral and anal phases. Freud argues that the child only knows one genital organ, the phallus, and that therefore boys and girls are opposite in the sense of phallic or castrated.

Freud introduced this term later to try to clarify the difference with the oral and anal phases, which were a bit disorganised. What Freud does say is that the primacy of the phallus is the most significant factor in this phase.

Penis envy is supposed to derive from this period when girls begin to realise they don't have one!

Freud's masculine bias comes out very clearly here as well since the whole apparatus of sexual development is discussed in terms of little boys. Girls are meant to be rather like boys only with a bit missing!

Boys and girls often seem to enjoy this phase however, being creative in playing with themselves, and noticing each other.

HANDS UP ALL THOSE WHO'VE DISCOVERED INFANTILE MASTURBATION!

This relatively innocent phase leads into the famous Oedipus complex (from 3-5)

Oedipus

The next important development is what Freud came to call the Oedipus complex (closely connected with the castration complex). All the development of infantile sexuality, its search for an object, comes to bear upon its parents. The secret desire to have sexual relations with the parent of the opposite sex is the basis of it all. There is also the corresponding hatred of the parent who blocks the way.

This relation to parents is what Freud claims makes the Oedipus complex universal. He named the complex after Oedipus because the story of Oedipus involved killing his father, marrying his mother and solving riddles. Freud was claiming to have solved the biggest riddle of all, the peculiarity of childhood sexual development and its influence on adult psychic life. The case of Little Hans brought out very clearly how his feelings for his mother and father represent what Freud meant by the Oedipus complex.

The Oedipal stage is where little girls become future women and little boys future men. The bisexuality that preceded the Oedipal stage Freud thought of in terms of active (masculine) and passive (feminine) drives. Freud claimed this distinction was fixed during the anal phase, either submitting or rebelling.

Freud looked at Oedipality through the lens of the active little boy, desiring his mother and threatened with castration by the father. This Oedipal drama is for Freud the very heart of the whole riddle of sexuality.

The resolution of the Oedipus complex in the normal way is that the child represses the whole thing and enters latency. How it is resolved and repressed re-emerges at puberty. The complex plays a fundamental part in the structuring of the personality and in the dvelopment of adult desire and behaviour.

Let's look at the case that Freud used as one approach to unravelling the riddle. Little Hans was a five year old boy who refused to go out because he thought horses might bite him. On the basis of one consultation and some discussion with the boy's father Freud pointed out that this fear was a product of the Oedipus complex. The argument went that Hans' father had a bigger penis then him, Hans had discussed "widdlers" with his father and had noticed that horses had large penises. Therefore Hans' fear of his father was displaced onto horses which might bite (castrate) him. Freud claimed that this case demonstrated for the first time that infantile sexuality could be seen in the infant rather than being deduced afterwards from adult memories. There were two problems with this case. One, that the client Little Hans reappeared fourteen years later with no memory at all of the events and two that Freud himself played a minimal role in it yet ascribed great importance to it.

However, Freud argued that the father was the proper person to do the analysis and that he was in fact the only one who could. This was to greatly affect child analysis later on.

The reason Freud considered it important was precisely that it demonstrated how a neurosis could be linked back to the formative Oedipus complex.

Little Hans felt castrated.

Another famous case that Freud quoted, was that of Sergei Pankyeff, a wealthy Russian aristocrat. He was, to put it bluntly, a bit of a mess. He wandered around Europe with his own doctor, looking for cures. Fortunately, he found Freud.

He was severely neurotic, anxious, dependent and compulsively searched for women with large buttocks who would pander to his particular sexual demands. He came to be called the Wolf Man because of his dream which supplied the key to his neurosis. In this dream he awakened one night to see the window open and several large white wolves sitting in a tree. He screamed and awoke. This dream began when he was about four and after this his real neurosis began.

For Freud the analysis of the dream demonstrated precisely what he had been arguing about childhood sexuality, about castration, anxiety and repression.

Just as in the Little Hans case – the origin of symptoms were childhood events.

All of this relates to the repression of desires that are too difficult to handle. The repressed Oedipal patterns become the unconscious material which shapes the normality or the neuroses of the adult.

What Freud argued was that the Wolf Man had in fact witnessed his parents engaging in sexual intercourse at an early age. This traumatic event, what Freud called the primal scene, led to the Wolf Man's neurosis, castration fears, obsessive behaviour and deep seated fear of the father. Freud subtitled his paper on the Wolf Man 'From the History of an Infantile Neuroses' and this both emphasised his interest in the Oedipal nature of the case but also indirectly attacked Jung's attempt to criticise such a position at the time. The Wolf Man was a very disturbed person and Freud worked with him for four years and was indeed much better at the end of it. For Freud it was proof positive of the theory of Oedipality.

SO WHAT DO YOU KNOW ABOUT THE OEDIPUS STORY?

IT'S THE GREEK GUY WHO DID IN HIS OLD MAN AIN'T IT?

I'M SURPRISED YOU ARE AWARE OF THE MYTH..

NOPE, IT'S TRUE, HAPPENED A WHILE BACK. HE CAME OVER FROM GREECE, HE WAS AN ORPHAN WHO JOINED THE MOB BACK IN CHICAGO...

IS IT THE SAME OEDIPUS WE'RE DISCUSSING HERE..??

MUST BE, WITH A NAME LIKE THAT. ANYWAYS HE GETS MESSED UP WITH THE BOSS, DECIDES TO SECRETLY RUB HIM OUT, THEN TAKE OVER AND RUN THE SHOW...

NOW YOU'VE LEFT ME BEHIND, HERR DETECTIVE.

AW, IT'S SIMPLE, HE WANTED TO BE THE BIG BOSS AND RUN THE CITY, TO BE THE GODFATHER...

THE GODFATHER?

THE MAN WHO RUNS THE MOB, THE BOSS OF BOSSES.

The Oedipus Quiz

1) Is the Oedipus complex universal?

2) Why is it necessary to use a myth to describe what is supposed to be an obvious human psychic reality?

3) Why should a child fear castration?

4) Why does sexual curiosity get repressed after the Oedipus complex?

5) Why did Freud never clearly define exactly what he meant by the complex?

6) Why is the positive form of the complex, the desire for the death of the rival, seemingly stronger than the negative form, love for the parent of the same sex.

7) How does the Oedipus complex work in societies where children are brought up, not by mother and father, but by the extended family, or uncles, or communally?

8) Why did Freud initially think there was a total symmetry between the development of boys and girls, and then decide the development of girls was more complex?

9) Why did Freud originally think the fear of castration came from real threats from parents and nurses?

10) Why did Freud later argue that the fear of castration came from hints, fantasies and, most importantly, from the little boy seeing the 'actually' castrated little girl?

11) What has sibling rivalry got to do with Oedipality?

12) Why are boys and girls supposedly the same but different in the Oedipus complex?

Psychoanalysis
BI-SEXUALITY

Womb	Mouth	Anus	Genitals

Primary patterns of feeling in the womb?	Oral Phase Love/Hate Rage/ Contentment Empty/Full Breast/ No breast Self love	Anal Phase Bodily Functions	Discovery of Phallus and Phallic sexuality
Start of anxiety?		Giving/ Withholding Creating Reflecting Aggression	Pleasure and masturbation
Leads to trauma of birth.			Turn to the external world.
	Narcissism Passivity		

BI-SEXUALITY
Polymorphously Perverse

Libido develops and is shaped

At A Glance
GENDERED IDENTITY

Oedipus Complex	**Latency**	**Puberty**	**Adult hood**
Child desires parent of opposite sex. This desire is repressed. Castration is the implied punishment for this desire and rivalry with parent of the opposite sex. Said to be the fundamental drama of human sexuality.

Repression. Boys and girls take separate routes. | Infantile sexuality repressed.

Amnesia.

Acquires social and cultural skills.

Boys and girls go their different ways.

No qualitative change. | Re-emergence of sexuality.

Oedipal resolution.

Difficulty of the sexual object.

Process of establishment of normal heterosexuality.

Girls can be fixated, regressed, fetishised. | 'Normal' sexuality of father's and mother's orgasm.

Heterosexuality.

'Male' and 'female' life of the Ego, Id and the Super-ego.

Neuroses etc.

Natural object of sexuality is meant to be intercourse. |

by these experiences.

'Normal' people develop into a sort of acceptable sexuality, but actually lots of people don't. Homosexuality, perversion, fixation, regression, neurotic repetition, all of these things can, and do, emerge out of the development of human sexuality. Elements of the different repressed phases merge into expressions of sexuality at puberty and one can be stuck (fixated) at an early phase, or regress to them.

Human beings are peculiar in the sense that our sexuality does develop in two distinct phases, the first set of which are repressed and yet shape our adult behaviour. It is Freud's discovery of this complex and difficult process that is so significant, and so often unacceptable to a sexually repressed society.

You might ask yourself why our society is so obsessed with sex but wants to deny childhood sexuality and anything that isn't 'normal'.

So now we have a model of how the human mind develops.

A Mechanical Interlude

In his analysis of the unconscious and of its manifestations in everyday life Freud implicitly worked with a model of the mind. In 1895 he set out a theory of the mind. (This is the Project for a Scientific Psychology we talked about on page 34).

Freud wanted to develop a model of how the mind works, both in normal and abnormal individuals. He tried, in keeping with his biological determinism, to show how the physiological and the psychological levels fitted together.

Freud's tinkering with abstract models of the mind was, to put it mildly, bold. There are real problems with these models, as Freud recognised. He changed and developed these models at different times in his life but still subscribed to the notion that ultimately there was a physiological basis to the whole thing. The idea that the mind was like a machine that sought to work efficiently in disposing of excess energy in very much a 19th century notion. Freud called it the Constancy Principle and it informs his approach in many ways. From the complex model in the Project Freud took those areas which might best throw light on the dynamic processes he was interested in. Freud's critics all say that the models he used were all too mechanistic and that they blinded Freud to the really difficult question about people's aims and intentions, not just the discharge of energy.

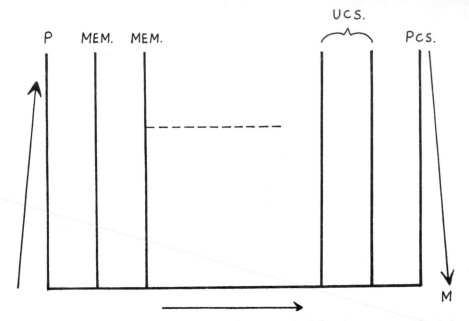

This model is from the *Interpretation of Dreams*. The left is the perceptual end, the other the motor end. This explains how dreams operate backwards from the motor end back to the precept that triggered the unconscious memory.

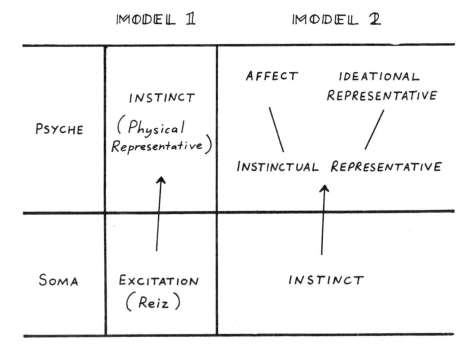

These two views are meant to represent how Freud thought the instinct operated in a technical sense. Model 2 is the later version.

91

Freud and the Psychoanalytic Movement

Once Freud had the basics sorted out he naturally enough wanted other psychiatrists to agree with him. Freud set out to build a psychoanalytic movement, quite deliberately and systematically. His worst critics in fact, claim he was a megalomaniac who wanted to create a religious order with him as the Pope. Freud felt that he was the guardian of the analytic psychoanalytic theory and practice, and that he would always be under attack because of the radicalism of his ideas, but he was never a tyrant. He often tried not to see dissension when it was there, with Jung, Rank, Adler etc but he could be harsh once he felt he had been betrayed. This, as he might well point out, is a fairly basic human reaction. Building a psychoanalytical movement was not easy though.

Freud often felt his endeavours went unrecognised. Certainly, his chances of an academic career were not great, being Jewish and a theorist of sexuality didn't help. Some of his colleagues made quite strenuous efforts to have him elevated to the rank of professor and he was nominated in 1897. Freud ignored the fact that he was passed over and refused to play the game of greasing the right palms. In 1902 he suddenly changed his mind and persuaded a Baroness friend to intercede with the Minister for Education. Within a couple of months he was signed up by the Emperor and was a registered professor. Apparently it cost a modern painting to persuade the Minister to act. We don't know what Freud thought of this carry on but it probably wasn't printable anyway.

Having become a professor, Freud seemed to have become properly ambitious and he never really looked back.

Freud goes to Hollywood

A Professor G. Stanley Hall of Clark University, Massachusetts, managed to persuade his university to award Freud an honorary degree. So in 1909 off went Freud and Jung to America to open a new chapter in the world history of psychoanalysis. Freud demanded, and got, extra money out of Hall to go and set off on this part-holiday, part evangelical mission. He was full of European prejudice about America and ambivalence about his reception. He gave five lectures which were quite well received, and constantly moaned about the food. He met William James, the psychologist and philosopher, and was generally well treated. Why, then, should he later say things like 'America is a mistake'?

It is also an interesting question as to why he fainted in Jung's presence before they left. (Not for the last time.) Freud said the answer was repressed homosexual feelings, but it may have been father – son stress.

The progress of psychoanalysis was hindered by the outbreak of the *1st World War (1914-1918)*. It brought personal hardship to Freud, reinforced his sense of pessimism about human nature and made him even more certain of the irrational basis of human behaviour. At the same time the 1st World War hastened the death of 19th century civilisation, brought psychoanalysis to the fore and ushered in the 20th century culture in which Freud was to be so central. In particular psychoanalysis came to be recognised as important in the treatment of war neurosis or 'shell-shock'. Ordinary treatments were clearly ineffective and so it came to be recognised that something else – something deeper, was at issue. Civilisation and its discontents now had to be reconsidered.

One of the effects of the war was that Freud rethought his theory of anxiety based on war neuroses.

Some geographical thoughts about psychoanalysis

It is too cold here for psychoanalysis.

Psychoanalysis is big in the States.

Argentina has many psychoanalysts.

Psychoanalysis, which started in Vienna, the home of the frivolous and decadent, spread very slowly to other German speaking countries, then to Zurich and Budapest. Only after the First World War did it really break out of Europe. America's early interest in psychoanalysis developed into a full-blown love affair. Freud never seemed wildly happy about it.

Psychoanalysis has a very limited history in Russia.

PSYCHOANALYSIS STARTED HERE.

Do the Chinese have Oedipus complexes?

Africa, where man started, never entered Freud's calculation.

Between the wars psychoanalysis hit Australia.

"THE COMMITTEE" 1922
BACK – OTTO RANK , KARL ABRAHAM , MAX EITINGTON , ERNEST JONES
FRONT – SIGMUND FREUD , SÁNDOR FERENCZI , HANNS SACHS .

In 1900 Freud gave a lecture at the University of Vienna. Three people turned up!

The psychoanalytical movement then grew out of Freud's Wednesday society, which met in his waiting room. Things started moving around 1902 and by 1910 Freud was getting to be well-known.

Otto Rank was the secretary of the Vienna Psychoanalytic Society from the start, and his minutes of the meetings tell us what fun they had. Right from the start there was acrimony and disagreement. The first International Congress of Psychoanalysis was held in 1908 in Saltzburg. The next year the International Journal of Psychanalysis was first published.

In 1910 Freud proposed setting up the International Psychoanalytical Association and the Viennese brigade opposed it. It was all downhill from then on!

In 1912 Jones proposed setting up a secret committee of those who were faithful to Freud, this inner circle was probably very influential.

Psychoanalysis turned out to be something that it was very easy to disagree about. Why this is so is in itself a very interesting question.

The psychoanalytic movement gained ground very slowly and from the beginning always felt on the defensive. It was attacked and slandered by psychiatrists, psychologists and by the press at large, which may explain why it took on the character of a religious sect. For a group that claimed to understand human behaviour it often displayed lamentable intolerance towards its own members.

The question of organisation loomed large from the very beginning, as did the question of lay analysis. Arguments about therapy itself, about the Unconscious, about which was best, Viennese chocolate or Swiss, kept them all occupied.

Ferenczi never completely got the order of the boot, but he did fraternise with Otto Rank and was interested in the short version of therapy. Basically Ferenczi was concerned about the length of time that analysis could take, several years somtimes and tried various ways of speeding the process up. Freud greatly disapproved but a final break never actually came, so perhaps Ferenczi shouldn't be included be included here. What was particularly interesting though was the way in which Ferenczi emphasised the 'inter-personal' nature of the therapy situation.

Wilhelm Stekel on the other hand was a regular bad guy from Freud's point of view and acyally said "After thirty years' experience of analysis I no longer believe in the overwhelming significance of the unconscious".

This really was heresy and the less said about him the better!

Alfred Adler (1870-1937) was one of the first to fall out with the orthodoxy. Adler was a member of the Vienna psychoanalytic society and appeared to be a happy protogé of Freud's. All this started to change in 1907 when Adler published his *Study of Organic Inferiority* in which he argued that 'to be a human being means the possession of a feeling of inferiority'. For Adler, early erotic impulses turned out not to be sexual, but aggressive.

He also argued that some original organ inferiority, that is, a biological cause, determined neurosis. Biology was destiny for Adler. Everyone seeks to compensate for some organic imperfection. This was clearly non-Freudian and it wasn't long before he was driven out. In 1911 Freud started to talk about how to 'force out the Adler pack' from the Psychoanalytic Society.

This was the beginning of a pattern.

Otto Rank (1884-1939) was another member of the group who began to diverge from the Freudian orthodoxy and paid the price.

Rank had been one of Freud's direct protegés From 1905 Freud had recognised

Rank's potential and had supported his academic education, in reality treating him as a son.

Rank was always a member of the Vienna Psychoanalytic Society and of the Committee when it was formed in 1912. For a very long time 'little Rank' as Freud called him was a well-behaved member of the movement. It wasn't really until 1924 that even Freud noticed something, and even then he didn't think Rank would be a real deserter.

In 1924 Rank and Ferenczi published a book *The Development of Psychoanalysis* in which they advocated the idea of shortening the period of analysis. This seemed to suggest that somehow the childhood experiences perhaps weren't all that important, and that the adult patient could quickly deal with problems. This of course was heresy, but worse was to follow. Rank, in his book, *The Trauma of Birth*, argued that the Birth Trauma, and the fantasy of returning to the mother's womb, was more important than the later stages of development. This was real heresy.

Basically Rank was saying the trauma of birth was more important than the Oedipus complex, and that anxiety stemmed from this terrifying event. Rank went off to the States in 1924 and told everybody about his birth trauma as though it was official psychoanalysis business. Freud told him off but still couldn't bring himself to give him the chop, and it was 1926 before Rank was eased out.

Freud's desire to build the psychoanalytic movement led him, one suspects, to be too optimistic about other psychiatrists who joined the ranks. Ultimately everyone who disagreed with Freud and left, or was thrown out, did so over the issue of sexuality. Jung was to be no exception.

Jung started off as the crown Prince, was, for a time, the President of the International Psychoanalytic Association, and then became another heretic. Freud possessed the truth and Jung deviated from it. Actually in retrospect the disagreements were there from very early on.

In a paper given in 1913 in London, Jung announced that he was going to free psychoanalysis from its overemphasis on sexuality and began to talk about 'analytical psychology'. This was the final break. Jung went on to develop his own psychology, which was clearly very different to Freud. Here's a typical exchange of views from the time:

ANNOUNCING

CARL "GOY" JUNG	VS.	SIGMUND "BOY" FREUD
• COLLECTIVE UNCONSCIOUS		• THE UNCONSCIOUS
• THE MIND (PSYCHE)		• INFANTILE SEXUALITY
• LIBIDO (DYNAMIC)		• REPRESSION
• OPPOSITONS (ENERGY)		• OEDIPUS COMPLEX
• PROGRESSION / REGRESSION		• DREAMS (AND WISH FULFILLMENT)
• SYMBOLS (PSYCHIC FACT)		• FREE ASSOCIATION
• SUPPRESSION		• SCIENCE (DETERMINISM)
• PERSONAL UNCONSCIOUS		• CASTRATION / PENIS ENVY
• COMPLEXES (CONSCIOUS / PARTLY CONSC.)		• CHILDHOOD AMNESIA
• ARCHETYPES (PRIMORDIAL IMAGES)		• SUBLIMATION
• MYSTICISM / MYTH		• NARCISSISM
		• INSTINCTS / DRIVES

Unfortunately Jung was still head of the International Psychoanalytic Association, having been put there by Freud. The congress of 1913 was a tetchy affair and not long after it Jung resigned as editor of the *Jahrbucher*, citing 'personal reasons'. Freud was worried that Jung might make off with 'his' journal and the International Psychoanalytic Association itself.

Fortunately Jung wasn't too interested and resigned as president of the International Psychoanalytic Society on April 20, 1914. Freud decided to write quickly a *History of the Psychoanalytic Movement* in which he would set out his version of all the dissension. To give an idea of how calm Freud was about it all, he called this work the 'bomb'. Having cleared out the trouble makers Freud wanted to clarify what psychoanalysis stood for and what was in opposition to it. It was the night of the wrong drives.

There is one revealing episode with Jung that hardly ever gets mentioned and that was his seduction of one of his patients, Sabina Spielrein. When he was confronted about this by the patient's mother Jung wrote back saying that since he wasn't being paid he shouldn't be expected to act professionally! Freud knew all about this but kept quiet.

Wilhelm Reich

All of these disputes about the nature of psychoanalysis revolve around how it interacts with other areas, like culture, society, history and, with Jung, mysticism and religion.

Freud always wanted to keep the social out of what he saw as his narrowly defined scientific field. Wilhelm Reich started out an orthodox Freudian but he later wanted to marry it to Marxism.

This was bound to lead to trouble and sure enough it did. He left the orthodox movement in 1933 and developed his own ultimately rather weird, theories about orgones, orgasms and things!

His early work on *Character Analysis* has been very influential. In this book he looked at the way external symptoms, like a habitual sneer or twitch, were a mode of expression of frequent emotional states. He talked about the way the character, the body, is repressed and moulded by society and about how sexual revolution was connected to social revolution.

He threw out Freud's theory of the death instinct and claimed that aggressive and anti-social behaviour were actually to do with existing social conditions, that is capitalism.

His attempts to combine politics and psychoanalysis led him to suggest worker's clinics, to help ameliorate social repression, and to work with the Communist party.

In another well-known work *The Mass Psychology of Fascism* he set out to analyse the rise of fascism and the causes of submissive behaviour amongst the masses.

The suppression of sexuality in young children he argued, led to a stunting of growth, to a crippling of the whole personality and to a submissive attitude to authority.

The Dictator he saw as a sexually maladjusted figure whose psychosis expresses the social maladjustment of an era.

The idea of sexual liberation and social liberation being connected was obviously influential in the 1960s.

What are the causes of all these divisions in psychoanalysis? Presumably, it was not simply a matter of the personalities of the various theorists, although it is true that a lot of them didn't like one another.

Here are some possible reasons to explain the endless splits in the International Psychoanalytic movement, in no particular order.

1) Because psychoanalysis is so difficult to understand, and to accept in individual terms, it is bound to produce disagreements. This is the repression reaction thesis.

2) Every change in the nature and results of therapy seems to throw a different light on theoretical explanations.

3) As soon as someone does disagree, rational discussion gets replaced by theoretical abuse and new 'schools' are formed, rather like religious sects. The purity of the doctrine has to be upheld.

4) There actually is fundamental disagreement about the basic concepts of psychoanalysis because of its complex and revolutionary nature. Any new science has to overthrow previously held ideas and that always involves a very difficult struggle in which violent emotions are roused. This is the cultural revolution thesis.

5) The dynamics of leadership always bring about disaffection and rebellion. This is the oedipal theory of theory.

6) The unresolved problems about social versus biological causation were also bound to cause splits since Freud himself veered towards the biological .

7) Possibly Freud was something of an authoritarian and insisted on his control and his theoretical line.

In reality Freud was always changing his mind about aspects of psychoanalysis, he just liked to pretend he didn't.

AGGRESSION IS ALSO PART OF THE OEDIPUS COMPLEX — IT'S NOT JUST SEXUAL.

I have to listen to the criticism of all these people, Adler, Jung, Rank etc. The point is that the models of libidinal energy, repressed sexual energy, don't explain everything. So it's Revision time. We'd better clarify the system into three parts.

ID (new name for the Unconscious.)

EGO

SUPER-EGO

Some revision notes.

1) Freud was always a determinist, which means whenever he is talking about psychic phenomena he considers it to be caused by some process in the dynamic system of personality.

2) The Id, the unconscious, is not that mysterious or impenetrable, it is part of normal life and psychoanalysis can demonstrate its effects.

3) When Freud talks about 'trieb' he doesn't mean instincts as many of his translators suggest, but drives, which are very different things. If it was all instinctual then Freud would be a biological determinist, but he's not.

4) Freud argues that too much repression of any kind leads to neurosis and unhappiness. This central fact determines much of modern civilization.

The First World War

The First World War made me think more clearly about internal conflict, aggression and human destructiveness in general.

War is certainly not pleasure and aggression seems to be more important.

I am interested not just in general neuroses, but in ways in which the libido is withdrawn from external reality, how it can turn in on itself. It is something to do with defence against the drives.

In 1914 Freud set out to write a new book of essays that would sum up the changes, but for various odd reasons it never appeared. Freud got stuck thinking again about why repression occurs. He moved back to thinking about the ego, but also going beyond some of the earlier formulation.

I THINK I FEEL SOME METAPSYCHOLOGY COMING ON ... THIS PRODUCTIVITY IS PROBABLY DUE TO THE SPLENDID IMPROVEMENT IN THE ACTIVITY OF MY BOWELS.

Some introductory writers on Freud give the impression that he has a simple view of sex as being at the core of everything. It must be clear to everyone by now that this is crude and underestimates what Freud means by sexual drives rather than sex itself. Within the overall framework of the structures of the mind and the patterns of development of the human individual Freud constantly revised aspects of the theory. In his discussion of Narcissism (1914) he once more set the cat amongst the purists. Freud was considering extreme neuroses and patients who did not respond to therapy at all. In order to explain these patients who seemed to be beyond the limits of language, and psychoanalysis is of course a talking-cure, Freud called on the myth of Narcissus.

This favourite greek myth of Freud's recounted the tale of a beautiful youth looking in the pond and falling in love with his own image. Loving himself proved impossible, he could not possess himself, so he pined away and died. He was then transformed into the narcissus flower. This simple image was a potent explanation of the ego that turns in on itself and can no longer communicate with the outside world.

Freud's adoption of this argument about narcissism and its importance was quite unexpected and even shocking for those who had understood his work simply as a theory of the conflict of drives.

I AM SO VERY BEAUTIFUL I WILL LOVE MYSELF, I DO NOT NEED TO TALK TO ANYONE ELSE... I WILL WITHDRAW FROM THE OUTSIDE WORLD.

I PUT THAT SO WELL

LOVE IS HIT OR MYTH

Narcissism is at heart auto-eroticism, which gets bound up with the ego and with language, there is no outside, nothing to react to. It is not the opposite of the sex drive but the same thing, the sexual object becomes the ego, there is no opposition, no dualism. Many post-freudians have taken up this notion and today some people talk about the Narcissistic society in which we live.

What makes the theory such a landmark in Freud's work is that it clearly seems to suggest that biological, or sexual drives, are no longer an adequate basis on which to work. Some say it represents a crisis in Freud's theory of the instincts. The old opposition of the sex drives versus the ego drives was broken down by the notion of narcissism.

> BUT IF NARCISSISM MEANS THE EGO DRIVES ARE SEXUAL THEN THE OLD DUALISM OF INSTINCTS IS GONE...

> I HAVE NO INSTINCT OTHER THAN TO BE IN LOVE WITH MYSELF. THERE IS NO CONFLICT

This precisely posed the question once again of where the repression of sexual impulses comes from. The opposition of the reality principle and the pleasure principle no longer seemed to hold. Ernst Jones for one found this mini-theoretical revolution a bit hard to handle. Freud more or less pretended it all fitted into the great pattern.

The old theory of instincts, the two great drives, for self-preservation and procreation, or hunger and love, ego and sex, weren't always up to the job of explaining everything. So in 1920 Freud had another go in *Beyond the Pleasure Principle*. Partly in response to an interest in war neuroses Freud began to think about this repetition compulsion...

Freud's introduction of this notion of the death-instinct, what he called Thanatos, was to explain aggressive and self-destructive tendencies he discovered in analysis. In a sort of return to the old idea of the Constancy principle he was arguing that there was a kind of biological drive towards embracing death. This idea was then counter-balanced by the life instinct which Freud then called Eros, the god of love. We are back with the old dualism that Freud loved so much.

The death instinct was never really accepted by many analysts and is now mostly regarded as speculative and possible the product of a deep pessimism.

Freud himself was unsure of the value of the notion of the death instinct, sometimes called Thanatos, in opposition to Eros, the God of love.

In as much as the death instinct was really discussing kinds of aggression and self-hatred, it was clearly an important analytic tool in therapy. As an explanation of war, suicidal intentions, drug-abuse, alcoholism and the sort of risk-taking that is suicidal, it is clearly an interesting approach. Lots of writers have found the idea intriguing but the scientific basis for the notion seems limited, as Freud was aware.

Whether the human personality seeks death as a kind of natural drive is a very tricky question, in fact some people argue that the opposite is true that the survival instinct is much stronger. Freud needed the death instinct however as an opposition to keep alive his beloved dualism once narcissism had flattened out the theoretical playing field.

In always trying to find the balance of forces at work in driving the human psyche Freud had to keep shifting his ground, In one sense he was always trying to keep the orthodox model rolling whilst incorporating all of the variations he came up against. This is what then led to the second topography, the dynamic system he brought out in 1923. The Id, the Ego and the Super Ego.

Now there are two more complicated things that come out of developments in Freud's theories of the mind.

First of all the realisation that to understand why ideas are repressed we need to understand instinctual drives and secondly we need to understand what Freud came to call the super-ego. (Freud proposed this new model in 1923.)

We know what the ego is, but what about the super-ego!

In classical theory the super-ego is the heir of the Oedipus complex, in that it is created through internalising parental prohibitions, or taboos. The super-ego applies the strictest moral standard to the helpless ego which is at its mercy. A feeling of guilt is the expression of the tension between the ego and the super-ego. The decline of the Oedipal effect leads to latency in which the super-ego develops. The existence of the super-ego is confirmed in the 'inner voices' that drive conflict in people.

Religion, morality and inner conflict clearly derive from the super-ego whose function can be socially manipulated, which, in effect, is what organised religion is. Kafka illuminated the sense of 'guilt' that every individual feels and which has a strange and haunting quality.

What is the origin of the super-ego?

Well, if you think about it, young children are amoral and posess few inhibitions against indulging their impulses. Parents provide the external power of control and so if you consider it carefully you will see that the super-ego is merely the internalised version of external constraint. The super-ego thus takes over the function, power and even methods of the parental agency.

The super-ego develops in line with the resolution of the Oedipal complex. For example, if there is an incomplete resolution of the Oedipus complex we find that the super-ego is stunted in its growth. The infant represses its desires and hatreds of its parents and defensively builds the super-ego.

The super-ego is also the vehicle by which the ego measures itself, and which demands perfection from the ego. So altogether the super-ego has the function of self-observation, of conscience and of maintaining the ideal.

The super-ego is then both a very important part of life and an important step forward in Freud's theories.

One of Freud's few comments about Marxism came out when he was discussing the super-ego.

"It seems likely that what are known as materialistic views of history sin in under-estimating this factor. They brush it aside with the remark that human 'ideologies' are nothing other than the product and superstructure of their contemporary economic conditions. That is true, but very probably not the whole truth. Mankind never lives entirely in the present. The past, the tradition of the race and of the people, lives on in the ideologies of the super-ego, and yields only slowly to the influences of the present and to new changes; and so long as it operates through the super-ego it plays a powerful part in human life, independently of economic conditions".

This discussion of the super-ego is very important in the study of group psychology and we'll come back to it with looking at Freud and society. Of course, some post-Freudians disagree about the super-ego and argue that it starts to develop before the onset of the Oedipus complex.

Whenever it starts, it presents a problem in analysing the dynamics of the personality. Its moral attacks on the ego can lead to anxiety. So let's have a look at that.

Individualism is a fantasy of bourgeois ideology, social man will be reconstructed under a revolutionary regime. Happiness is a worker's party.

Freud got worried about the problem of anxiety because it was such a generalised phenomenon.

Anxiety is, of course, a very important concept in psychoanalysis, playing a central role in bringing attention to problems within the personality. Anxiety is a form of fear and obviously can vary enormously from mild anxiety to acute phobia. Freud described 3 types of anxiety:

1) Reality (objective)
2) Neurotic
3) Moral

Anxiety as a state feels the same in all 3 cases but the point is where that anxiety comes from. Roughly speaking the cause of anxiety for Freud in these cases is

1) The real world (war, crime etc.)
2) The Id (Nasty, instinctual feelings that demand fulfillment.)
3) The Super-ego (or conscience). One is threatened with being punished for a moral transgression.

Feeling anxious then is the ego's way of telling the individual that there's a problem. The anxiety state could come from a mixture of all sources, psychoanalysis has to try to work them out. Feeling guilty, or anxious, is something that seems more common in industrial society than previously.

Mourning and Melancholia

In a further extension of the ideas around narcissism Freud also looked at *Mourning and Melancholia* (1915).

Self-hatred perversely enough begins in narcissism, withdrawal from the world turns the ego in on itself. Depressive illnesses like melancholia (a middle-ages word for severe depression), resemble mourning gone berserk.

The lost object (parent/lover etc), is 'introjected' and turned into a bad object. The super-ego punishes the helpless person who 'blames' him or herself for the loss of the 'bad' object. Self-destructive impulses can multiply if contact is lost with reality and suicide becomes a real possibility.

For Freud these self-destructive tendencies were very much to do with the previously mentioned death instinct. Some claim that the doom and gloom around him prompted some of these arguments.

FREUD

MARX

EINSTEIN

After anxiety, the Id, the Ego and the Super-ego, the main dynamic model of psychoanalysis was in place. Super-ego and society were the two main problems in the general sense that remained, to which we'll return.

What Freud had established as a model of the human being was a highly complex dynamic system of energy, controls, repression and releases, which drove the average human being through mainly instinctual drives. The reality principle simply held in check the power of the Id – the unconscious, and attempted to mediate the complex demands that derived from an individual's pattern of psycho-sexual development. The id wishes or acts while the ego tries to hold it all together. From infant sexuality to adult neurosis, via everyday life, repression, resistance and sublimation, is a long and tricky ride. Freud's revision of his theories he simply saw as adding further elucidation to the basic outlines that for him never changed. (See p40 - 100) Sex, love, aggression and fear are the motors of Freud's dynamic system and it is his insistence on the baser instincts that make him unpopular with the moralists.

If we had to summarise Freud so far we would have to say that he presents an extremely radical, dynamic view of the human subject, which takes sexual development in its widest sense as the basis of the dynamics of personality. The inter-action of the Id, Ego and Super-ego, grounded in biology, is the fundamental reality of human psychology for Freud.

Freud and Society

Freud's analysis of human nature and human behaviour developed into a full blown social anthroplogy. What had started as a new medical procedure had become a sociological mode of analysis. Freud set out to broaden the scope of the application of psychoanalysis. Freud had always argued that civilisation required repression.

In *Totem and Taboo* (1913) Freud tried, by using anthropological evidence, to consider how all human kind had developed from primitive peoples to higher civilisation.

From Darwin had come the hypothesis that primitive man had lived in a primal horde in which, like animals, one male was dominant.

Young males were forced out of the group and young females were controlled by the father figure. Freud felt that this was an historical account of how primitive society developed and used it as a basis for his speculation. How accurate it is, is difficult to say. (Is it a scientific myth?)

What we can say is that Freud is using Oedipal theory to produce social analysis. Freud argues that the young males rise up and murder their father in order to get Women and that this primal murder is the founding of civilisation.

Having murdered the father they are overtaken by a terrible sense of guilt and a need to expunge it. Hence through sacrifice and the creating of a totem (like religion), the guilt is controlled and social relations made possible. The origins of the super-ego lie here in internalising the guilt of killing the father. The role of the leader (father/fuhrer) is also very important for Freud.

This scenario is often attacked as not being historically true, or being totally mythological, or both.

It is best to treat it as a metaphor about social order and psycho-sexual relations. (Or Patriarcher II in which the baddies do over Schwarzenneger.)

All of this discussion is about how groups function and how sexuality is organised and controlled within the group.

Instead of direct sexual expression, one-to-one, the group is formed through sublimated relationships, most importantly, through the father figure.

In other words to become properly social we have to repress some of our initial desire. The one-to-one love relationship with the mother must be broken into by a third term, the father.

So we start off in love with ourselves (narcissism). Then we love the mother, recognising ourselves as a separate person. Then we have to identify with a wider social group.

We often take on an ego-ideal, someone we would like to be (Madonna or Sylvester Stallone).

Our behaviour in groups is very much psychologically similar to mob group behaviour. Leaders seem to be necessary, like fathers, to make it all work.

Freud was recognised as, and sometimes acted like, the father of psychoanalysis. He was however, human, made mistakes, and had foibles and addictions like everyone else.

Freud and Politics

Freud's relationship to politics was always equivocal, but also distant. His hatred of Nazism is clear but his reluctance to recognise what was happening, and to do anything about it, is a little odd. He said, " I do not believe that Austria left to itself would degenerate into Nazism". In fact the Austrians proved themselves better Nazis than their German teachers. Vienna in 1933 after the German invasion was swept by violence, anti-semitism and spontaneous attacks against jews which stunned many observers. Freud was reluctant to leave; he was after all, old, established and internationally famous. It was only with a great deal of persuasion and international pressure that he was prised out of Vienna, and only just in time. The Nazis burnt his books, of course, which led him to comment that since in earlier centuries they would have burnt him as well, then this must be progress.

For someone who understood religion so well it is strange that Freud understood politics so little.

In looking at Freud the man it is difficult to go past his little habit of smoking. It is not clear when he had his first cigar (6 or 7?), but once he started he seemed completely unable to give up. His advice to a nephew of his was "My boy, smoking is one of the greatest and cheapest enjoyments in life, and if you decide in advance not to smoke, I can only feel sorry for you". This oral obsession may explain why Freud himself paid little attention to the oral phase, he hardly wanted to talk about his addiction. In 1923 Freud developed a growth in his mouth associated with smoking, and promptly kept it quiet. He, and others, always managed not to talk about it openly, despite the fact it was cancerous. This started a very long series of operations on the jaw and plastic jaw devices to replace a rotting jawbone. His speech became impaired and he was often in pain, and operated on, but he kept smiling, as they say.

This was an addiction.

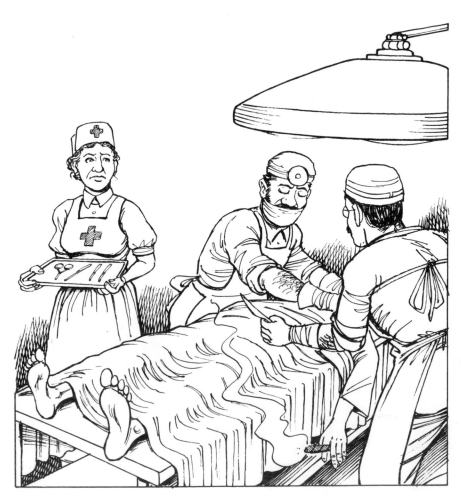

Freud died in his new Hampstead home suffering greatly from the effects of his cancer of the jaw. He died on September 23 1939, a few weeks after the Nazis invaded Poland and began that slaughter which was once again to demonstrate the irrationality of man and his capacity for evil. To Freud this was perhaps not an unexpected eventuality, but to the optimists of Western Europe it was to be a fatal blow. Freud's analysis of civilisation and its discontents became more pertinent than ever. Freud died as he had lived, stoical, critical, in control and without a hint of sentimentality or illusion. His ghost haunts our culture.

Freud always had a very high opinion of science and a very low opinion of human nature. He was probably half wrong on both counts.

But he was at least consistent.

The key questions he left were the relationship between the Unconscious and society and the debate about 'masculinity' and 'femininity'.

"I find women difficult to understand – although I am perfectly able to analyse what they really think. That was the problem with Dora – she wouldn't listen to my interpretation".

Queer chaps, women, as somebody once said.

Freud on Masculinity and Femininity

130

What do Women really want?

The path that little girls' sexuality takes is meant to be very different to that of the boys'. (So said Sigmund).

Whereas little boys fear their father and castration, little girls have to take the opposite path. They discover that they are already castrated.

Both sexes take the mother as the primary love object. Little boys confront Oedipality by repressing the desire for the mother and transferring it into a desire for another woman. He puts off becoming like the father until adulthood.

The little boy, fearing castration, concedes the power of the father and takes his place in normal culture.

The little girl, discovering she is already castrated must deal with her 'mutilated' condition, wondering why her mother has brought her into the world in 'this shape'. She turns on her mother, develops 'penis envy' and turns to the father for consolation. Her desire for a penis turns into love for the father, and the desire to give him a baby, a sort of penis substitute. Thus the little girl becomes hostile to the mother, submissive to the father and narcissistic, as well as masochistic. Freud also later said women lack a sense of justice due to the 'predominance of envy in their mental life'.

Oh boy, oh boy, as they say. Oedipus has got a lot to answer for.

Many feminists have profoundly disagreed with Freud's analysis of femininity and have accused him of supporting a patriarchal view of women as inferior.

On the face of it this seems like a justified accusation. His 1931 lecture on Femininity is not a very good defence; it seems wholly to support the idea that women are, by nature, passive, masochistic, envious of the male, less rational and with a weaker super-ego.

Why women should be a mystery to Freud is itself something of a mystery, since psychoanalysis is supposed to be about understanding human beings. He himself in his essay says that what he has to say is 'certainly incomplete and fragmentary and does not always sound friendly'. When you consider just how much Freud wrote, the fact that he did write so little about women speaks volumes about his own position.

It is easy to see why feminists, and others, object to Freud's analysis of femininity. He absolutely seems to be saying that *biology is destiny*.

Penis envy and passivity seem to be the lot of "normal women, there's no freedom for the feminists

It is not surprising that many critics have denounced Freud as a patriarchal old fart and have dissected his corpse to reveal his fear of women written on his heart, (they then put a stake through it).

Frankly, his view that women are inferior is just wrong and may be the result of what has come to be called 'womb-envy'. That is men's deep-rooted hostility to women because at the end of the day they hold the ultimate power of creation, of giving life and they are the mother as well. It is boys' lack of power rather than the possession of the penis that is central. However, the relationship between Freud and femininity is not simply one of rejection. The theory of psychoanalysis provides a starting point that could be describing what tends to happen, rather than what has to happen. Freud can be seen to be describing masculinity and femininity as they existed in 19th century bourgeois society. Freud is basically the starting point for much of today's discussion about masculinity and femininity, in the sense that the child's development into the adult is still the central riddle of humanity.

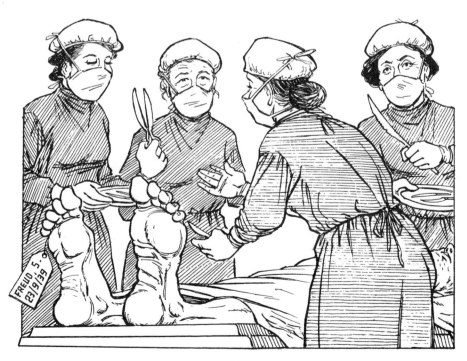

What Freud always claimed to be was objective, but the argument is that he was so bound by his own outlook as a male that he mistook prejudice for science.

The basic equation of male/active and female/passive is something of a Sigmund complex that probably has to be got rid of before proper discussion of sexuality can be developed.

Right from the beginnings of psychoanalysis there was disagreement about masculinity and femininity, particularly from women analysts. Some of them, like Anna Freud, remained pretty orthodox, however.

The defence counsel for Freud might well say that he had entered such new territory, that he couldn't be expected to get everything right. He did, for example, recognise that 'masculine' and 'feminine' were very difficult terms and that everyone started off bi-sexual.

Return of the Repressed

PROTESTORS IN HYDE PARK YESTERDAY BURNED THEIR BRAS ... COL.5

Psychoanalysis in the United States was mainly orthodox and even reactionary in its acceptance of the 'anatomy is destiny' line and because of this the modern generation of feminists not unnaturally turned on Freud. Post-2nd World War American society was preoccupied with ideas of natural motherhood and maternal instinct. Freud's claims about feminine passivity and masochism, and women's supposed diminished sense of justice, were used to justify this return to the family.

Many feminists, however, threw out penis envy, biological determinism and women's passivity as simply justifications for male domination. This era of the sixties was mythologised in popular culture as the 'bra-burning' time, although there is little evidence that such a strange activity actually went on.

Kate Millet *Sexual Politics*, Betty Friedon *The Feminine Mystique,* Shulamith Firestone in *The Dialectic of Sex* and notoriously, Germaine Greer in *The Female Eunuch* all developed standard feminist critiques of Freud.

They all addressed a similar question: 'How could Freud pontificate about women's passivity when women had never had the chance to overthrow it?' If male domination was the case then women were oppressed, not naturally passive. Masochism could be seen as the result of imprisonment rather than a 'normal' attribute of femininity. The question of political power, of cultural domination, was back on the agenda, counter-posed to Freud's biological determinism. In fact, culture versus biology keeps popping up all over the place. Freud's famous patient Dora, who basically seems to have refused his interpretation of her 'problem' has prompted huge debates in this area.

It may be the case that this generation of feminists threw the Freudian baby out with the biological bath water, but the tide has turned again. Juliet Mitchell in *Psychoanalysis and Feminism* took a more sober view and set out to rescue and reconstruct Freudian theory for feminism.

Non-biological Freud with a pre-oedipal emphasis, and added non-patriarchal analysis seems like a much better bet.

Nancy J. Chodorow set out to consider the implication of psychoanalysis for feminism or how understanding Freud could help in understanding male domination. Unlike Freud she certainly does not accept the notion that male is the natural order of things. Talking about masculinity she argues that it is in effect a defensive, insecure category. She argues that women's mothering generates this defensive masculine identity and also a compensatory psychology and an ideology of male supremacy.

We ain't scared of nuffin, except our mum.

We can say that masculinity is aggressive precisely because it is insecure. This kind of approach was not available to Freud since he seemed to assume that sex roles were more or less biological and that women were the 'weaker' sex. Freud completely failed to understand the male fear of women or its cultural institutionalisation. What Chodorow was looking for was an explanation for the virulence of masculine anger, fear and resentment of women. The suggestion is of course that men resent and fear women because they experience them as powerful mothers. This pre-Oedipal relationship is more important than Freud's emphasis on Oedipality and the father.

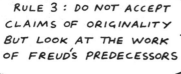

RULE 3: DO NOT ACCEPT CLAIMS OF ORIGINALITY BUT LOOK AT THE WORK OF FREUD'S PREDECESSORS

PEOPLE HAD TALKED ABOUT DREAMS OF THE UNCONSCIOUS BEFORE?

OF COURSE THEY DID!

LOOK AT E. VON HARTMANN'S "PHILOSOPHY OF THE UNCONSCIOUS".. 1868, AND I THINK FREUD PROBABLY READ IT...

UH-HUH, INTERESTING

SOME OTHER PSYCHOLOGIST, MR. EBBINGHANS SAID OF FREUD'S THEORIES "WHAT IS NEW IN THESE THEORIES IS NOT TRUE, AND WHAT IS TRUE IS NOT NEW"

NICE, I LIKE IT..

ANYWAY, RULE 4 WITH FREUD FOR BEGINNERS IS: BE CAREFUL ABOUT ACCEPT- -ING ALLEGED EVIDENCE ABOUT THE CORRECTNESS OF FREUD'S THEORIES; THE EVIDENCE OFTEN PROVES EXACTLY THE OPPOSITE.

Eysenck's objection to psychoanalysis can be summarised as follows. (See *The Rise and Fall of the Freudian Empire.*)

1) Because psychoanalysis is not quantifiable, nor falsifiable, it is not scientific.

2) Freud's scientific sample base, his patients, was far too limited and specific to be adequate. (His patients were mostly middle/upper class Jewish women of a neurotic/hysterical persuasion.)

3) Freud's work does not contain much hard data, in fact it is often merely alluded to. There is no way of checking his interpretation therefore.

4) Freud was unscientific in collecting his data. He saw 4-5 patients a day and wrote up his notes in the evening, the accuracy of which must be questioned.

5) Freud was against quantification (statistics) which produces vagueness.

6) Without statistics it is impossible to analyse whether observations arose by chance, or can be correlated with similar events.

7) Psychoanalytic theory is not refutable (Karl Popper), which is the very essence of scientific theorising. How can you adduce contrary evidence for the life and death instincts?

8) Psychoanalytic theory cannot predict, it can only explain after the event.

9) Therapy does not actually work very well. Eysenck argued that in fact therapy in many people delayed recovery. Other research has shown that all kinds of therapy have roughly similar (placebo?) effects.

10) Psychoanalysis is simply mythical fantasising dressed up as science and belongs with alchemy, theosophy and other mumbo-jumbo.

Eysenck is particularly annoyed that any attack on Freud is simply treated as evidence of repression of the unpalatable 'truths' of psychoanalysis.

If there's one thing that annoys me, it's behaviourism and pedantry.

145

Anna Freud

The infantile ego fears the instincts because it fears the outside world, ie objective anxiety.

Anna was Freud's favourite daughter, his social secretary, nurse, pupil and eventually a psychoanalyst herself. Freud doted on her and even analysed her, which still surprises many people. Interestingly, she never married, or had many particular engagements of the emotions with other sexes. One may speculate about this.

She did, however, become an important member of the International Psychoanalytic Association, defending the orthodox position of psycho-therapy.

Her best known work *The Ego and the Mechanism of Defence* (1937), emphasised her tendency to attach more importance to the ego, or conscious mind, than in fact Sigmund did.

What she insisted on was looking at the ego's unconscious defence mechanism, the way in which the ego tried to defend itself against internal and external forces. In the main these forces are,

1) The power of the instincts (the return of the Id).

2) The punitive power of the super-ego.

3) Threats from the external environment (particularly in the child).

Anna saw herself as simply extending her father's work and got fairly cross with anyone she thought was messing with the truth, like Melanie Klein.

Melanie Klein (1882-1960)

FREUD FORGOT ABOUT THE CHILDREN.

Melanie Klein emigrated to England in 1926 and worked with Ernest Jones. What she also did was to pay a good deal more attention to children than Freud had done.

She, and the rather mysterious Hermoine von Hug-Hellmuth, who was murdered by her nephew, developed a whole new branch of psychoanalysis. This was child analysis. Freud hadn't really thought it was possible but Klein developed a play therapy that allowed her to treat children as young as 2.

Freud was somewhat sceptical about Klein's work and thought Ernest Jones was conducting a campaign against Anna Freud by supporting her. In fact Klein's work with infants was highly significant and after Freud's death some in England saw her as the successor to Freud.

Melanie Klein also gave more importance to the very early phases of infant development – the pre-oedipal. Orthodox Freudians for example, thought the super-ego didn't develop until the dissolution of the Oedipus complex at about the age of four.

Klein insisted that earlier psychic life was much more important than Freud had realised.

If you allow infants to play freely you can understand their psychic life

It is odd how Sigmund and Anna resist this important advance.

The Object-relations School

Going right back to where Freud talked about the difference between the sexual aim, the desire to do something, and the object, who or what you wanted to do it to, we can look at this post-Freudian school of thought.

Melanie Klein and D W Winnicott are the two important people here, being the originators of this approach.

As we have already seen with Melanie Klein the important difference with Freud is that she wants to go further back into infantile life than does Freud. What she argues is that there is no instinctual life that does not involve object-relations. What she means by object-relations is precisely that it is always towards something, an object, a person, a thing that mental life is orientated. It is not the aim that is important but the object and how we deal with it, or internalise it.

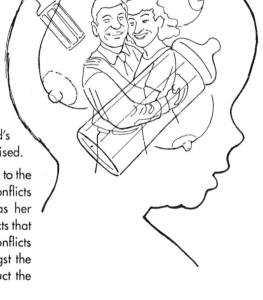

Klein claims that object-relations are central right from birth and that therefore Freud's theories of stages has to be revised.

Basically she pushes right back to the earliest infant life all of the conflicts that beset the adult, taking as her model the life and death instincts that Freud talked about. These conflicts are lived out internally amongst the inner 'objects' that we construct the world out of.

What the object-relations analyst is interested in is precisely those 'objects' or 'figures' that the individual internalises. From the very beginning, the baby battles it out through good and bad objects. We might say that this approach is anti-theoretical in that it sticks to the clinical evidence. Anna Freud didn't like it at all.

The Two Heavyweights in Child Analysis

ANNA FREUD v MELANIE KLEIN

(Orthodox side)	(Advanced side)
Totally orthodox but emphasises the ego and its defences. Oedipality is the central issue:	Fairly orthodox, but claims to have opened up the new region of the pre-oedipal.
1) Environmental factors, like parents, influence unconscious and instinctual factors.	1) Environmental factors are less important in psychic development than previously thought.
2) Sexual drives most important.	2) The important drives are the aggressive ones.
3) The Super-ego develops after oedipality.	3) Forerunners of the super-ego can be seen in infancy (0-2).
4) Only older children are analysable.	4) It is necessary to analyse infants to resolve early conflicts.
5) Parents are consulted and involved.	5) Parents are not involved because the child's fantasy life is more important.
6) The child's ego is seen as undeveloped and therefore uncontrolled. Interpretation is therefore difficult.	6) Fantasy life through play is the central fact of analysis.
7) The child does not develop transference.	7) The very early sexual and aggressive instincts involved.

The British it is well known do not like metaphysics, nor any sort of theoretical speculation. They are also individualistic, prone to eccentricity and rather fond of seeing themselves as objective. Hence orthodox Freudianism was attractive in one sense – its concern with the individual, but unappealing in its theoretical sophistication and insistence on sexuality. The British are rather repressed altogether, which is what makes them reserved, and they much prefer facts to fantasies. At the same time there is an obsession with smut and saucy stories in the press that demonstrates precisely how repressed sexuality operates in the culture at large. Funnily enough Freud liked England and the English took to him, perhaps because they shared an obsession with bad food, indigestion and dogs.

Oddly enough it was Melanie Klein's object-relations theory, or reworking of Freud, that actually became dominant in England. D W Winnicot has also been quite a big hit with the English.

Karen Horney (1881-1952)

The Post Freudians divide up very neatly into a sort of left-wing and right-wing. On the left we have the socialist influenced types interested in social and individual change and on the right we have the ones influenced by biology, who go ever further back into infant experience (The Kleinians).

It is the inevitability of anatomy versus the influence of the environment. This is one of those arguments that run throughout all human sciences, and never seems to get solved.

Karen Horney played on the left-wing, and it is claimed that her trainer was Alfred Adler, the socialist and trouble-maker whom Freud had to kick out of the Movement, for deviation from the orthodox.

Horney herself practised as an analyst in Berlin in the 20s and 30s and remained an orthodox Freudian. It was when she moved to the United States and became a staff member of the New York Psychoanalytic Institute that she began to develop an interest in social factors. She eventually parted company with the main Freudian body and ended up as the Dean of the new American Institute for Psychoanalysis. Her book *The Neurotic Personality of Our Time* sums up her differences with the traditionalists and like Adler's, is written for the general reader, not experts. .
All of her many books had this populist tone and were quite influential in America.

In essence Horney abandoned the fixed, determinist approach of classical Freudianism and adopted the view that cultural evaluation played a far more important role in producing neurosis than previously thought. She clearly recognised Freud's contribution to developing psychoanalysis but argued that he was locked in a 19th century mind-warp. In particular in relation to the differences between the sexes, Horney argued that Freud never escaped from anatomy and biology. Freud's anti-feminism she pointed out, lay in his biological notion of instincts, his insistence on immutable phases and his dualism. Masculine and feminine for Freud are mechanical opposites enshrined in biological history.

Horney is also anti-Oedipus in the sense that she does not accept that the Oedipus complex is universal or all powerful. This also leads her to argue that there is in fact no such thing as a universally 'normal' psychology. Rather she argues that there is culturally mediated social and psychological development.

In her *New Ways in Psychoanalysis* she sets out how these changes might work and how psycho-therapy might react to them. This approach definitely is post-Freudian in the sense that her analysis of psychic structure is quite different to Freud's.

Horney's position on women was quite simply that their 'inferiority' derives not from their 'castration' but in their understanding of their real social oppression. Women have been denied the patriarchal power that the penis represents but this is not, for Horney, a natural order of things, it is a social construct. Biology isn't destiny, it's an excuse, just as colour isn't a problem, it's a justification. Horney was clearly on the side of those who saw human nature as changeable, rather than fixed.

Juliet Mitchell in *Psychoanalysis and Feminism* attempts a much more complex operation, to rescue Freud from the accusations of biologism and to demonstrate that he does offer the basis of an analysis of masculinity and femininity. She draws on Levi-Struass to argue that the oedipal situation was universal in the sense that it derived from the incest-taboo and its role in the formation of society, (see *Freud and Society*.) Fundamentally Mitchell is arguing that although the oedipus complex still exists, based as it is on the origins of society, the exchange of women, it does not need to exist in modern society. Men used to exchange women between biological families in order to maintain the incest taboo but this is now simply redundant, although Mitchell says that these ancient laws of exchange are embedded in the unconscious. Those who disagree with Mitchell, and quite a few do, say that she doesn't provide any explanation as to why women are exchanged or why the father has power. The primal myth is not very convincing since it appears to be no more than that, a myth. Also if the oedipus complex can be destroyed it would suggest, like Horney, that it is not universal, or biological.

Modern Psychoanalysis

Psychoanalysis is really big business today, particularly in America. Popular versions of psychoanalysis are found everywhere in our post-modern culture. The language of psychoanalysis has become such common currency that it almost seems like common-sense, but real understanding is probably as distant as ever. Actually of course there are as many versions of psychoanalysis today as there are airlines. They all cost the earth and take off in thousands of directions. The 'new-age' we live in is centrally concerned with individual fulfilment and growth and psychoanalysis lurks behind every kind of therapy going.

The most dramatic change of course, has been the advent of feminist psycho-therapy in which old Freud's ideas about the inferiority of women have been somewhat questioned. From Juliet Mitchell's *Psychoanalysis and Feminism* to Chodorow's *Feminism and Psychoanalytic Theory*, everything is up for grabs.

As we have said, psychoanalysis as a general theory has been massively influential in the social sciences, in cultural theory, in sexual politics and in our attitudes towards individual development and behaviour. Despite fairly basic agreement about things like the existence of the Unconscious, of the importance of childhood etc there are a bewildering number of schools and disagreements within modern psychoanalysis. It sometimes seems that the unconscious motivations that drive human behaviour seem to be worse in psychoanalysts than in anyone else. Wherever ten psychoanalysts gather it seems to be a law of the Unconscious that there be at least five schools.

This is too idiotic for any decent insanity.

In America the American Psychoanalytic Association first of all split with the European over 'lay' analysis; that is whether you needed to have a medical training first. Then the whole movement split into two camps.

In 1956 the Academy of Psychoanalysis was formed which consisted of several smaller groups who had all disagreed with the authoritarian nature of the original association. Karen Horney, Harry Stack Sullivan and Erich Fromm were some of the big names in this split which came to be known as the 'culturalists' versus the 'Freudians'.

This 'culturalist' v 'orthodox' divide influences many other areas of debate. In particular over the usefulness of Freud for analysing all cultures and societies. Freud claims that the Oedipus complex is universal, the absolute basis of all human nature. Others however, say that different cultures produce different forms of psychological make-up.

In the 1920s and 30s anthropologists took a more serious look at primitive cultures. Amongst many others Malinowski and Mead did work which seemed to question Freud's model. Looking at the Trobriand Islanders Malinowski pointed out that the father played no role at all in bringing up the child and from this he inferred that the Oedipus complex was not in fact universal. The ways in which human cultures deal with the problem of infancy and growing to adulthood may be related to the unconscious processes of becoming an individual, but to claim the process is universal does seem reductionist.

Kardiner and others have in effect argued that different personality structures can be found in different societies. Margaret Mead furthered this attack on the Freudian notion of a fixed personality with her work on the differences in sexual behaviour in various tribes and cultures in the 30s. In her work *Coming of Age in Samoa, Sex and Temperament in Three Primitive Societies*, Mead points out that cultural differences extend across the whole personality and are not superficial. Child-rearing patterns are, even from a Freudian viewpoint, fundamental to shaping the personality and so it seems credible that vastly different patterns will produce different personalities.

From a more politically acute angle Franz Fanon criticised the inherent racism of much European 'colonial' thought which placed 'natives' in much the same sphere as women and children. Nineteenth century thought assumed the natural superiority of western thought and considered it universal, and in this Freud was as guilty as most. Fanon argues that 'it is a question of the Third World starting a new history of man'.

Freud's relevance to modern society is very evident when one tries to think about racism and identity. Just as masculine identity can be seen as insecure and always being defined as other than feminine, so racial identity can itself be seen as problematic. White means being 'not black' and the fear and hatred that constitutes racism can be seen as having psychological roots in insecurity.

In childhood black is associated in many western cultures with fear, evil, dark and wickedness. This unconscious symbolism is confused in adult life with reality, and racism is the result. The unconscious dimension of racism is shown in its irrationality and phobic nature, just like a neurotic complex or any other mental illness.

J Lacan (1901-1981)

In the squally history of psychoanalysis Jacques Lacan stands out like Moby Dick in a duck pond.

Starting out as a disciple he ended up usurping the father and playing Moses (mostly to the structuralists).

Lacan and his work are, without doubt, difficult to understand, some would say impossible. He is, however, still a Freudian and can only be understood if you first understand Freud.

For reasons that may, or may not, become apparent, Lacan writes in a manner that does not, like Freud, lead to a clear set of positions. It is odd that Lacan claims to be leading a back to Freud movement when he seems so implacably opposed to the kind of naturalistic science that Sigmund was so fond of.

Lacan is definitely one for the contradiction though. He is a structuralist, a linguist, a semiotician, a literary critic and philosopher and occasionally an analyst.

Lacan famously said that the Unconscious is structured like a language.

This shows 3 important things about Lacan.

1) He believes in the Unconscious.
2) He is very interested in language.
3) He can sound simple and clear whilst simultaneously being obscure and difficult.

(How can the Unconscious, home of the elemental, be structured like a language?)

We don't know whether Freud and Lacan actually met but we do know that they both published interesting things in 1938.

On the left we have Freud publishing *An Outline of Psychoanalysis*, a classic exposition of his somewhat old fashioned ideas and on the other side we have Lacan publishing an article on 'The Family', in which he elaborates ideas that go well past anything Freud may have thought.

Where Freud leaned towards biology and determinism, Lacan is interested in language and structures. Where Freud looked to the inter-relationship between biology and mind, Lacan wants to look at culture, language and mental structures.

Not to put too fine a point upon it Lacan modernises Freud through linguistics and tries to produce a universal psychoanalysis that rids Freud of his 19th century legacy.

Lacan was of course expelled from the International Psychoanalytical Association fairly early on for disagreeing with the orthodoxy and he eventually set up his own school (from which he expelled himself in the end).

Not only does Lacan engage in a baroque linguistic rhetoric that makes *Nostradamus* seem clear, he also went in for algebraic formulae that add up to the clarity of Hades.

Where Freud eventually set up a triadic structure of the mind – the Id, the Ego and the Super-ego, Lacan creates the trilogy of the Imaginary, the Symbolic and sometimes, the Real. (What connection there may be we'll come back to later).

Lacan starts off agreeing with Freud that the infant world provides the basics for later identity. Like the ingredients of a soup the fantasises and aggression of an infantile consciousness are mixed to produce a human subject, through language. For Lacan we don't live in a world of realities, but a world of signs, of signifiers. (A signifier is something that represents something else.)

When Lacan says that the Unconscious is structured like a language he means something akin to the fact that the unconscious works through metaphors and signs and representation. Rather as dreams do.

Lacan goes further than saying that the Unconscious is like a language. He says that before language there isn't any Unconscious. When the child acquires language it thereby becomes a human subject and enters the social world.

The first major difference between Freud and Lacan is that Lacan introduces something he calls *The Mirror Phase*. (see below)

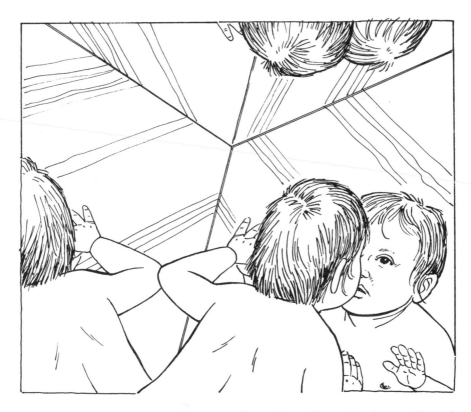

What this idea is about is that the messy infant, who is all over the place in physical and emotional terms, suddenly discovers an image of itself as whole, coherent and wonderful. That is that the human infant arrives at an idea of itself as an identity. It imagines itself as this coherent being it sees in the mirror.

This step forward means that the infant acquires a sense of self from outside, which is merely a reflection of itself. This false sense of self, this mis-recognised identity, is for Lacan a split that stays with the individual forever. We luxuriate in this imaginary sense of ourselves that the mirror gives back to us. It is the mother of course who reflects back to the child this coherent sense of identity, this reassuring sense of being. For Lacan this identity is wholly false and to work with it as a sort of ideal ego, he thinks is totally wrong. The true self is the unconscious self.

This mirror phase comes between 6 and 18 months and precedes langauge, Oedipality and all that other kind of stuff. Lacan talks about the universe that the child occupies in this mirror phase as the 'imaginary'. Unfortunately for the infant and everyone else concerned, in this world of the imaginary the mirror image is apparently a 'Signified' and the child itself is a 'Signifier'. How it got to be this and what it means derives from the structural linguistics of good old Saussure. (See *Philosophy For Beginners*.)

Fundamentally Saussure talked about how language worked as a system, how words derived their meaning from the system as a whole, how structure was important. Lacan takes this whole apparatus and plonks it down on top of traditional psychoanalytic theory. Thus it is that a baby can become a 'Signifier'. A sign you see can be seen as two parts, the Signifier and the Signified. The one is the word or the object eg the penis – the sign, the other is the thing it represents – the Signified eg the phallus/sexual power.

Saussure's revolution was to point out that there was no necessary connection or relation between the two things; the word and the external reality it represented.

Lacan marries structuralism and psychoanalysis to give us a MkII Freud in which psychic structures and linguistic structures have a complementary role. But whereas Saussure argues there is no fixed relation between a given Signifier and Signified,

Lacan, as a Freudian, wants to hold on to her idea that the penis inevitably symbolises the sexual power of the father/all men. It is the primary Signifier.

Just as language operates as a system, so Lacan argues society operates through a series of interrelated signs, roles and rituals. This order he calls the 'Symbolic Order'. Lacan's rewriting of Freud becomes most obvious here where he discusses the resolution of oedipality as entry into the Symbolic Order, the law and rule of the father.

So language as the Symbolic Order constitutes the universe of the child, and this order penetrates to the unconscious as well. Hence the dictum the unconscious is structured like a language. Acquiring language means assuming an identity, which is already split (mirror phase) but which is constructed by the Symbolic Order, the law, the language of the father.

The male child enters language and the symbolic order through resolution of the oedipal crisis and in so doing identifies with the father, the patriarchal order of the phallus. The phallus is for Lacan the Primary Signifier, the place of power in language, through which the Symbolic order is imposed. Clearly if the phallus is the source of power in language and being, then women are excluded and castrated; the law of the father silences femininity.

In fact Lacan argues that women are permanent outsiders, the other who cannot be a whole identity in a repressive world of language and discourse.

So we have this strange phenomena of the radical Lacan rewriting Freud through language and yet ending up with a position in which anatomy is destiny, only now (langanatomy) the word is imprisonment.

Reality becomes the prison house of language for Lacan and we are all forever doomed to wonder the halls of the imaginary or the symbolic in search of ourselves. It's no wonder we need therapy.

Post-Lacanians

Despite the contradiction between Lacan's seeming radicalism and what seems to be a reactionary position in relation to women, who are condemned by the language of the father, he has been very influential. Luce Irigaray is a psychoanalist who attempts to liberate what she takes to be the possibility of a feminine language from the male discourses of writers like Lacan. Although Lacan did talk about the 'jouissance' of feminine pleasure that existed but could not be spoken within patriarchal discourse, he hardly discussed how it would be liberated. For Irigaray

the Imaginary is the place where this potential might well exist. For Lacan you will remember the Imaginary is a prison of illusions in which false identifications delude the subject into a unity which is false. Boys however escape into the Symbolic Order there to enjoy the fruits of patriarchal power. Girls are left behind in the oedipal stakes and are therefore condemned, argues Lacan, to ignominy in the Imaginary. Irigaray however argues that this place in the Imaginary is not just a place of silence, of negativity, but a sphere of possibility, of a language that is not mediated through masculinity, or male power. Irigaray also argues that patriarchal thought has never been able to understand women, literally to think them, since language has been as Lacan argues, so symbolically male, the language of the father.

In her *The Sex Which is Not One*, Irigaray analyses western philosophy and psychoanalyses and systematically unearths the 'sameness' which she finds in patriarchal thought. This sameness is precisely that male gaze which can only see women as half-men, as men with a bit missing, as beings who are the negative of man, the other. In this vein Freud is as guilty as others and one must agree with Irigaray that his inability to understand women is more than accidental.

Julie Kristeva perhaps has the same aims as Irigaray but has a very different approach to the questions of masculinity and femininity. She draws on Lacan to talk about that pre-oedipal stage that she calls the 'semiotic' in which she argues there is the potentiality of poetic revolution which is repressed by the Symbolic order. Turning Lacan on his head, or disfiguring the nature of domininant discourse, Kristeva pits the power of the 'semiotic' against the symbolic. 'Woman as such does not exist', Kristeva argues, 'she is in the process of becoming'. Oddly enough Freud might not have dissented that much from such a sentiment.

NOW I WANT TO ASK YOU IF YOU FOUND ANYTHING ODD IN SIGMUND FREUDS OWN LIFE.

THERE ARE TWO AREAS THAT PRESENT PROBLEMS; SELF ANALYSIS AND ANNA FREUD

I MEANT ANY SORT OF SECRETS ... MURDER OR MAYBE COCAINE DEALS

DESPITE ALL THE STORIES AND RUMOURS, FREUD WAS A HIGHLY CONVENTIONAL, MORAL, LAW ABIDING CITIZEN, EVEN A BIT OF A BORE ...

WHAT ARE THE PROBLEMS THEN — INCEST?

TAKE IT EASY — THE PROBLEM WAS THAT HE ANALYSED ANNA WHICH WAS A BIT ODD, AND THAT HE ANALYSED HIMSELF WHICH WAS SORT OF AGAINST ALL OF THE RULES ...

AH, SO HE DID BREAK THE RULES

WELL I GUESS SO, BUT HE MADE THEM IN THE FIRST PLACE, SO IT'S PROBABLY OK

WHAT WE EMPLOYED YOU TO FIND OUT IS WHY PEOPLE TAKE HIM SO SERIOUSLY ...

OF COURSE, GENERAL, IT TELLS YOU LOTS ABOUT HOW AUTHORITY WORKS, HOW DISCIPLINE OPERATES AND ABOUT STRESS AND PSYCHOLOGICAL WARFARE. IT ALSO EXPLAINS WHY PEOPLE GO TO WAR AND HOW VIOLENCE ERUPTS

NEXT YOU'LL BE TELLING US FREUD CAN EXPLAIN MEN & WOMEN

NOT PERFECTLY BUT TAKEN AS A MODE OF THEORETICAL EXPLANATION FREUD IS THE BASIS OF AN UNDERSTANDING OF MASCULINITY & FEMININITY

I THINK YOU'RE SAYING THAT FREUD THEORY IS AS IMPORTANT IN A SOCIOLOGICAL SENSE AS IN A THERAPEUTIC ONE

FREUD IS IMPORTANT IN FILM STUDIES, MEDIA STUDIES, GENDER ANALYSES, WORK ON THE FAMILY, IN CRIMINOLOGY; ALL THE HUMAN SCIENCES IN FACT..

FREUD FOR BEGINNER 1ST DRAFT

PRECISELY PROF, HIS IDEAS ABOUT CULTURE AND SOCIETY ARE NOW ACCEPTED ... INDEED THEY HAVE ACTUALLY BECOME A PART OF OUR CULTURE ...

THAT'S ABOUT THE STRENGTH OF IT — THAT'S WHAT MY REPORT HERE SAYS, ANYWAY...

"...Or, to be free, mankind must know itself — illusions are the enemy of freedom"

Bibliography

Freud and General

Adler, A. *Understanding Human Nature* (1927)
Bocock, R. *Freud and Modern Society* (1976)
Brennan, T. *Between Feminism nand Psychoanalysis (1989)*
Brown, J. A. C. *Freud and The Post-Freudians* (1961)
Chodorow, N. J. *Feminism and Psychoanalytic Theory* (1989)
Crowley & Himmelweit. *Knowing Women* (1992)
Eliot, A. *Social Theory and Psychoanalysis in Transition*
Fine, R. *A History of Psychoanalysis (1979)*
Freud, S. *New Introductory Lectures on Psychoanalysis*
Freud, S. *A General Introduction to Psychoanalysis*
Freud, S. *On Sexuality* Pelican Freud. Vol 7 (See collected works)
Fisher & Greenberg. *The Scientific Credibility of Freud's Theories & Therapy* (1977)
Firestone, S. *The Dialectic of Sex* (1970)
Gallop, J. *The Daughter's Seduction: Feminism & Psychoanalysis* (1982)
Gay, P. *Freud* (1992)
Hall, C. S. *A Primer of Freudian Psychology* (1954)
Horney, K. *Feminine Psychology* (1973)
Jones, E. *The Life and Work of S. Freud* (1954)
Kline, P. *Fact and Fantasy in Freudian Theory* (1981)
Klein, M. *Collected Works* (1954)
Kristeva, J. & Rose, J. (eds) *Feminine Sexuality: Jacques Lacan & The Ecole Freudienne* (1982)
Irigaray, L. *This sex which is not one* (1985)
Lacan, J. *Ecrits* (1977)
Laplance & Pontalis. *The Language of Psychoanalysis* (1973)
Lasch, C. *The Culture of Narcissism* (1979)
Mannoni O. *Freud: The Theory of the Unconscious*
Marcuse, H. *Eros & Civilisation* (1969)
Miller, J.B. *Psychoanalysis and Women* (1974)
Mitchell, J. *Psychoanalysis and Feminism* (1974)
Mitchell, J. *The Selected Melanie Klein* (1986)
Ricouer, P. *Freud and Philosophy* (1970)
Skinner & Cleese. Families and how to survive them (1983)
Stafford-Clark, D. *What Freud Really Said* (1965)
Storr, A. *Freud* (1986)
Timpanaro, S. *The Freudian Slip* (1976)
Voloshinov, V.N. *Freudianism: A Marxist Critique* (1976)
Wollheim, R. *Freud* (1971)

Glossary

This glossary of terms sums up the main concepts used in this book.

ABREACTION: Describes the process of releasing a repressed emotion by reliving in imagination the original experience

AETIOLOGY: This means the investigation of the causes of a given phenomenon or series of phenomena: medically, the investigation of the cause of a disease or diseases.

AFFECT: Any kind of feeling or emotion attached to ideas or idea-complexes.

AGGRESSION: Opinion differs widely on whether aggression is a basic instinctual drive. Related to the death instinct and the opposite of the life instinct.

CATHEXIS: Accumulation of mental energy on some particular idea, memory, or line of thought or action.

COMPLEX: A cluster of ideas with a strong emotional overtone; the process whereby a complex becomes buried in the unconscious part of the mind is called repression.

Any constellation of ideas which are associated with strong feelings in a person's mind can properly be called a complex; they are usually memories of real or imaginary experience, together with the conclusions which the subject has reached about them, and the intense feelings which they have produced. May on occasion emerge partly or wholly into the preconscious areas of the mind; although it is the object of the repression to prevent this.

CONDENSATION: Term used to describe partial fusion of two or more ideas, occuring particularly in dreams, and producing a characteristic type of distortion, illustrated by such words as 'treaty of Breast-Litovsk'.

DEFENCE: Process of protecting the ego from anxieties derived from real or imaginary threats. Defensive action may modify the id's demands.

DISPLACEMENT: General sense, transfer of an object from one place to another: the shifting of affect from one item to another to which it does not really belong, particularly in a dream.

DISSOCIATION: The breaking off of connexions of any kind, in any sort of combination; used in special sense, originally by French school of psychopathology, for a functional interruption of associations or connexions in the mind, upon which the revival of memories and systems of ideas depends, as well as the personal control normally exercised over various motor processes, and producing forgettings, hallucinations (negative), anaesthesias etc, and generally the phenomena produced by Freudian repression.

DREAM WORK: Idea that the dream content consists initially of the various sensory impressions received by the sleeper during sleep, together with the worries of the previous day, and exciting experiences mainly of the recent past. Freud argues that to this content repressed trends or wishes from the unconscious tend to attach themselves, but in order to evade the censorship, and fulfil the dream function which is to fulfil the wish to sleep, these trends and wishes modify the existing content, so that they may disguise themselves, the modification taking place in the unconscious.

EGO: An individual's experience of him/herself or her conception of her/himself, or the dynamic unity which is the individual. Psychoanalysts use it in an objective and narrower sense, of that part of the person which, as superficial, is in direct touch with external reality, is conscious, and includes, therefore, the representation of reality as given by the senses, and existing in the preconscious as memories, together with those selected impulses and influences which have been accepted and are under control.

FIXATION (psychological): The attachment, generally interpreted psychosexually, to an early stage of development, or object at such stage, with difficulty in forming new attachments, developing new interests, or establishing new adaptations.

HYSTERIA: Nervous disorder characterised by dissociation, high susceptibility to auto-suggestion, variety and variables of psychogenic, functional disorders; by psychoanalysts classified as a psychoneurosis arising from conflict and repression, where the repressed impulses and tendencies are expressing themselvess in the various symptoms etc, which the patient shows, certain characteristic varieties being specially designated anxiety hysteria, conversion hysteria, fixation hysteria.

ID: Employed by Freud to designate the impersonal mass interacting energies or forces constituting the unconscious a strict sense, or what might be designated the structural unconscious, behind the processes making up conscious life, as inner determinants of these processes.

LIBIDO: Term, used by psychoanalysts originally, in its usual sense of sexual desire, but later, in the most general sense of vital impulse or 'energy'.

NEUROSIS: A functional disorder, psychogenic in origin, of the nervous system, rather indefinitely marked off from psychoneurosis; regarded by psychoanalysts as a conflict phenomenon, involving the thwarting of some fundamental instinctive urge.

ONANISM: Producing the sex orgasm by manipulation, or other artificial stimulation of the genital organs.

PSYCHOANALYSIS: Basically a method of treatment of mental and nervous disorders, developed by Sigmund Freud, characterised by a dynamic view of all aspects of the mental life, conscious and unconscious, with special emphasis upon the phenomena of the unconscious, and by an elaborate technique of investigation and treatment, based on the employment of continuous free association.

PSYCHOGENESIS: The origin and development of mental phenomena in general, or particular features or peculiarities of mental processes, as manifested in behaviour.

PSYCHONEUROSIS: Term usually employed, though not always consistently, for the group of functional nervous or mental disorders, less serious and less fundamental than psychoses, of which hysteria may be taken as the type.

PSYCHOSIS: Abnormal or pathological mental state, constituting a definite disease entity; term applied at one time generally to any mental state or process as a whole; a deteriorative psychosis is a psychosis showing progressive loss of mental function.

REGRESSION (psychoanalytical): Reverting of the libido to a channel of expression belonging to an earlier phase of development, or the reverting of the individual to interests and forms of behaviour characteristic of an earlier or infantile stage, often as a result of fixation.

REPRESSION: A conception developed by Freud and the psychoanalysts which has largely displaced the idea of dissociation, the essential difference from dissociation being that it is dynamic and explanatory and not merely descriptive; applied primarily by Freud, to a mental process arising from conflict between the pleasure principle and the reality principle, as when impulses and desires are in conflict with ordinary standards of conduct; as a result such impulses and desires are actively or automatically thrust out of consciousness into the unconscious, in which, however, they still remain active, determining behaviour and experience, and producing neurotic symptoms of various kinds. It has been suggested that the term repression should be employed in its ordinary sense of 'actively thrusting out of the mind', and the term suppression employed for the automatic process, to which the term is practically restricted by Freud.

SCREEN MEMORY: A psychoanalytic term for fragmentary memory items from early childhood represented by something trivial in processes of condensation, in the manifest dream content. Sometimes called cover memory.

SEX: A fundamental distinction, relating to reproduction, within a species, dividing it into two divisions, male and female, according to which sperm (male) or ova (female) cells are produced. In psychoanalytic theory sex and sexuality are widened so as to include phenomena which have no direct bearing on reproduction, on the assumption that the pleasure derived is of the same order, is in fact essentially the same, in the case particularly of the young child, as that associated with sex phenomena in the strict sense; if in such cases sensuous were substituted for sexual, many of their views would be more readily accepted.

SUPER-EGO: Term employed by psychoanalysts to designate a structure in the unconscious built up by early experiences, on the basis mainly of the child's relations to his parents, and functioning as a kind of conscience, criticising the thoughts and acts of the ego, causing feelings of guilt and anxiety, when the ego gratifies or tends to gratify primitive impulses.

SYNDROME: A complex going together of the various symptoms of a disease; a symptom-complex.

TRANSFERENCE: Term employed by psychoanalysts of the development of an emotional attitude, positive or negative, love or hate, towards the analyst on the part of the patient or subject; also used generally, of the passing of an affective attitude or colouring from one object or person to another object or person connected by association in the experience of an individual person or animal.

TRAUMA: Any injury, wound, or shock, most frequently physical or structural, but also mental, in the form of an emotional shock, producing a disturbance, more or less enduring, of mental functions.

UNCONSCIOUS THE: Freud's original term used to designate those processes which were not knowable by the subject. Psychoanalysis is based on the discovery of the unconscious, its laws and methods of gaining access to it. Chater renamed the Id to specify its function as the site of instinctual drives.